Graphics Essentials
for Small Offices

Graphics Essentials for Small Offices

David Loeff

SciTrans
Colorado

Loeff, David

Graphics Essentials for Small Offices
Includes figures, glossary and references
ISBN-13: 978-1461052135
ISBN-10: 1461052130

1. Graphic design — handbook, how to, basics.
2. Document design. 3. Small business marketing.
4. Marketing communications. 5. Computer graphics basics.

Graphics Essentials for Small Offices

CONTENTS

What's in this handbook

Every organization faces challenges, and these can arrive in different forms depending on an organization's size and structure. For an organization housed in a small office or home office (SoHo), the ability to implement new ideas and change directions quickly may be offset by its size. Size imposes limitations on staff, space, budgets and time. While a larger organization may have an in-house graphics department, a smaller organization may have to choose between hiring out graphic tasks or using existing staff to perform them.

It's not uncommon for staff members in small organizations to perform many roles. A SoHo employee may, for example, answer phones, greet visitors, keep the books, and mail out correspondence. Asking such a multi-tasker to take on graphics as well does not seem unreasonable; however several factors should be taken into account: Does this person have adequate knowledge to do the job properly? If not, how much time will it take for this person to acquire the knowledge? How much time will it take away from performing other duties? Will operational inefficiency result when time is taken away from mission critical activities?

On the other hand, hiring out graphic design can be expensive. Additionally, what you need may not be what you get. For example a graphic designer who is used to working for large corporations may deliver a product requiring expensive printing on costly paper unless your budget has been made clear from the start. If the person who makes decisions regarding graphics isn't familiar with all the options available, unnecessary costs can arise.

Many publications are available which provide step-by-step guidance to specific software. This handbook doesn't do that. It is for hands-on people who acquire software skills quickly. Therefore, my emphasis is on the principles of graphics rather than on step-by-step guidance. This is a condensed overview of graphics that concentrates on generally applicable techniques, rather than on those which require specific software. My goal is to provide the basic knowledge you need to create good looking graphics, avoid common mistakes, and save money on your graphics budget.

The first chapter of the handbook, **About text and graphics**, briefly discusses graphics in its historical perspective and the current need for basic graphics knowledge. The need to project a sense of mission and organizational identity is discussed next. The chapter ends with a discussion of how to create a graphics budget.

The following chapter, **Typefaces and fonts**, addresses type anatomy, history, measurement, and type mistakes to avoid. Using type attractively is discussed in the chapter on **Text spacing: alignment, leading and kerning**.

Whether you outsource your graphics or perform them in-house, a little knowledge can go a long way. Basic computer software and digital printing equipment is not expensive, but it can have its limitations. If your printing is done in small quantities, you may be able to get by with off-the-shelf solutions. But when printing quantities become larger, savings can be gained by using a commercial printing company. In the chapter on **Desktop Publishing packages**, I discuss some of the limitations of low cost software and how to get around them.

Principles of good design is self-explanatory, while **Working with images** addresses color models, equipment profiling, the differences between graphic file types and the appropriate use of each.

The chapter on **Photo editing** provides basic tips, while **Planning your project and getting it press ready** provides guidance for ensuring error free output. A comprehensive glossary and reference list concludes the handbook.

About text and graphics

Every written, printed, or online communication consists of two components — text and graphics. Although the text of a written communication is important, it isn't the entire communication. How the written text is arranged, its size, color, and weight constitutes the **graphics** component of a communication. The appearance of a written communications is its graphics. A graphic designer is someone who specializes in making sure that the appearance of a communication complements and enhances its textual component. A designer's efforts often result in a written communication that is more easily readable.

The two textual elements of graphics are **typography** and **layout**. However, graphics consists of other visual elements as well. Typically a graphic designer also creates or chooses illustrations and photography, logos, and other decorative elements used in written communication.

A minimal use of graphics

Consider an imaginary organization — one that communicates solely through letters. Graphics is not a strong concern for this organization. After all, a letter is a letter. But the person who types the letters still needs to make some decisions about their appearance. For example, how close to the top of the letter should the body of the letter begin? How many lines should separate each paragraph? Should each line have a consistent width or should some variation be allowed? These are graphic choices.

During the typewriter era, few graphics options were available. You could set right and left margins and make limited choices regarding the space between lines. But, that was about it. Typically, only one font was available. It wasn't until late in the typewriter era that changeable fonts became available.

Graphics Essentials for Small Offices

Today, every computer ships with a wide choice of fonts. And every letter can involve a number of choices that weren't available during the typewriter era. Today administrative assistants make choices that were once made by graphic designers. Yet, most have never had training in graphics.

Every letter on a typewriter has the same dimensions. This means that every keystroke produces a letter that is as wide as every other, and each letter is spaced an equal distance from every other letter.

If you examine a line of a **monospaced** font such as Courier, you'll have a pretty good idea of what typewriter output looks like. Although Courier is available as a computer font, people usually prefer to use **variable-width** fonts (**Figure 1.**).

Back when computers were pricey and huge, typewriters were still the main option for typing text. When an organization wanted to have a document professionally printed, it typically employed a graphic designer. Some designers had their own typesetting equipment; others employed professional typesetters. Designers would sketch out rough thumbnails of how they wanted the finished document to look. Then they created layouts that represented finished documents. Finally, the designer would choose a font or fonts for the text areas of the document.

Since every font is a unique size, designers would estimate how many characters could fit into an inch and multiply this estimate by the width of the area in which the type was to fit. Then the designer had to estimate the number of type lines that were needed to fit within the text area. Often, the estimate didn't work out the first time around. Then the designer had to decide if he wanted to use a different type size, or change the layout dimensions or typeface. Once these details had been worked out, he could instruct his typesetter regarding how to set type.

A monospaced font

If you examine a line of a monospaced font such as Courier, you'll have a pretty good idea of what typewriter output looks like. Although Courier is available as a computer font, people usually prefer to use variable-width fonts.

A variable-width font

If you examine a line of a monospaced font such as Courier, you'll have a pretty good idea of what typewriter output looks like. Although Courier is available as a computer font, people usually prefer to use variable-width fonts.

Figure 1. Monospaced and variable-width fonts

5

Graphics Essentials for Small Offices

Today, word processing software automatically does much that typesetters used to do. However, it can't do everything. That's part of the function of specialized publishing packages such as inDesign and QuarkXPress.

You don't need an expensive desktop publishing package, however to begin thinking like a graphic designer. There are low cost alternatives to high-end publishing packages that you can use to create professional-looking documents. Even basic word processors have capabilities that allow them to produce excellent results. The key to creating good-looking documents isn't necessarily owning the best software and equipment. Rather, the key is learning some basic graphic design concepts and putting those concepts to best use.

The intentional communicator

Organizations write mission statements because they help to clarify their purpose and the means of achieving their purpose. It's certainly possible to run an organization without a mission statement, but it helps to have one. A mission statement defines your identity and can serve as a moral compass. As a mnemonic aid, a mission statement can remind you to stay on mission, or redirect you if you begin to drift off course.

Mission statements are one aspect of how organizations express their identity. Organizations can express themselves through traits, character and mood — often intentionally, but sometimes unintentionally. An organization may consider itself dependable, cheerful and trustworthy — and demonstrate these traits through its behavior. Other organizations may be two-faced, unpleasant and conniving while pretending to be otherwise. Such organizations make positive statements about themselves but fail to support their statements with appropriate behavior. Such organizations may survive, but aspects of their reputations will suffer. In the end, the members of these organizations fool themselves more than they fool their public.

The best way to define your identity is to consciously state your values and deliberately describe the behavior required to support those values. Organizations create unique personalities when their members know who they are, and what they stand for. An organizational personality is an asset which can supply purpose to an organization's internal and external communications. Your organizational personality creates bonds among your members and a presence in the community.

What I call organizational personality is similar to, but not the same as, corporate culture. The manner in which members of an organization perceive themselves and present themselves to others is fundamental and tied up in identity and personality. Corporate culture describes broader aspects of organizations, such as whether the organization encourages risk or minimizes it, how it defines its leadership and rank and file, whether its ideas are innovative or result from groupthink, etc. Although small organizations can, and do, have cultures, they tend to be more informally defined than the cultures of larger organizations. That's why I prefer to discuss organizational personality, or how an organization's members behave and present themselves to one another and to the public. The personality your organization presents to the world constitutes its identity and much of its individual brand. Every member of your organization should know its purpose and behave in a manner consistent with its identity.

Once an organization's personality is known and understood, it can become a component of your communications. What you say, how you say it, and how your message appears — all contribute to establishing your organizational identity. For this reason, you should establish and maintain a general communication style, composed of both written and graphic components.

Two fundamental practices can go far in projecting an organizational persona. The first is the adoption of a standard writing style manual such as *The Chicago Manual of Style* or *The Associated*

Press Stylebook. The use of style manuals assures consistency, and consistency helps reinforce identity.

Second, ensure consistent graphics by using a **corporate identity manual**. This manual will consist of your logo, variations of your logo (including all permissible color schemes), your letterhead, envelopes, and business card design. Identity manuals also specify the typefaces your organization uses, how these typefaces are used, and their weights and styles such as normal, bold, italic and bold italic. Guidelines regarding color use should also be included.

Consider your organization's personality and mood when designing a corporate identity manual. Ask these questions: What does this font say about my organization? Does it say we're cheerful, serious, reliable or friendly? What does this color say about our organization? Is it vibrant and speedy or deliberate and careful? How does it combine with other colors we might use? Can we define a set of colors we can use throughout our communications in order to demonstrate a consistent identity? Do we also want to define a sub-set of colors to use when we wish to convey a specific type of message?

If this seems like too much to think about, just give it your best shot. Organizations change and adapt over time and you don't have to know all the answers during your first go around. It's not unusual for major corporations, with well recognized branding, to periodically review and redo their identity graphics.

The communications audit

Every organization needs to know the costs of providing its goods or services. In addition to material and labor costs, administrative and promotional costs also need to be considered. Some tasks generate income directly while others fill supportive rolls. For example, in a manufacturing environment, those who build products (labor) are considered to have a direct relation to income. Those who perform tasks such as accounting and marketing (administration and promotion) do not directly generate income, yet they serve essential functions. A manufacturer needs to know his direct manufacturing costs, his indirect costs, and his overhead.

In smaller organizations, it's not unusual for employees to perform both income generating tasks and supporting tasks. This makes assigning costs somewhat trickier than in an organization where employees perform either income generating or supporting tasks.

Let's assume that you know Joe Employee spends 75 percent of his time generating income and the other 25 percent of his time performing administrative tasks. What happens when he gets assigned a graphics project requiring 50 percent of his time? Now Joe spends 75 percent of his time generating income and another 50 percent of his time working on the graphics project. Where will the extra 25 percent of Joe's time come from, and who will perform the tasks Joe dropped in order to work on the graphics project?

If you don't want Joe getting stressed out, you need to know how much time he can reasonably allocate to graphics tasks. This is especially true if you happen to be Joe. If Joe doesn't know how to retouch photos for a company publication, should he take the time to learn Photoshop, or is it cheaper to let Joe do something else and pay a vendor to retouch the photos? How about in the long run? If Joe learns Photoshop now, will it save your organization money in the future? There are no one-size-fits-all solutions to problems like these. Every organization has different assets and different needs.

In addition to assigning personnel to graphics projects and estimating their labor costs, other costs need to be considered. You also need to know how much you plan to spend on the non-labor costs of communicating graphically. In addition to the cost of design, costs for such items as photography and printing can burn deep holes into budgets. I recommend performing a communications audit when planning for your next fiscal period.

Such an audit should answer these questions:
How do you communicate?
How often do you communicate?
How many people do you reach with your communications?
What is the per-unit cost of communicating?

How do you communicate? Communication can take many forms — from posting flyers on telephone poles to advertising on television — and everything in-between. Perhaps the bulk of your business comes from phonebook ads and phone queries. Perhaps, it comes from radio advertising, from your website, or from referrals. Regardless, you need to know where your mouth is before you can put your money there.

As you list your communication methods, consider the effectiveness of each versus its cost and the amount of effort it requires. Do some of your methods provide too few results for too much effort? Do others provide greater results with less effort? Are there opportunities you've overlooked because they seemed too complicated? Maybe they're less complex than you thought.

How often do you communicate? Is your newsletter published quarterly or monthly? How often do you post new information on your website or blog? Is the frequency too often, too seldom, or is it just about right? Why do you think so?

How many people do you reach with your communications? If you're trying to sell a house, will you need 10,000 flyers or are 50 or 100 enough? Since a house can only have one buyer, you might choose to match the volume of flyers to the volume of weekend drive-by traffic. On the other hand, if your business depends on volume, you may want to print a greater number of brochures or catalogs.

Along with how many people your message reaches, you should also consider how suitable are the people you reach. Reaching a lot of people randomly does little good if they are not part of your desired demographic. Offering exterior painting to every resident of a townhome complex makes little sense. You need to reach the handful of board of directors who make the actual painting decisions. Nor does it make sense trying to sell automatic garage doors to high-rise apartment dwellers.

What is the per unit cost of communicating? Determine what you can afford to pay to send your message to one person when planning your overall communication budget. For example, if it costs a dollar to mail a four-color newsletter to one person, and you receive a $50 contribution for every hundred newsletters mailed, your printing costs will exceed your revenue. If you decide instead to mail cheaper, single-color newsletters that only cost 25 cents apiece instead of one dollar, than your printing costs will only be half of your revenue. On the other hand, if 100 copies of a two dollar brochure results in the sale of a half-million dollar home, than your printing costs are negligible.

Determine your communication budget for the upcoming cycle by understanding how much money you receive each time you deliver one unit of goods or services, how many units need to be delivered each cycle, and how many prospects must be reached in order to create demand for one unit of goods or services.

Printing costs can vary widely depending on how many colors are used, how many copies are printed, the type of paper used, and its sheet size in relation to the finished size of the printed item. Whether the printing is done on a digital or traditional press will also affect cost. Digital printing works well for small quantities because it doesn't involve the costly setup time that traditional presses require. On the other hand, traditional presses run much faster than digital presses.

Graphics Essentials for Small Offices

Since setup costs are absorbed into the overall press run, as the printed quantity increases, the cost per piece decreases. Quantity savings are far less dramatic when the printing is digital.

Have a budget in mind before undertaking a graphics project yourself or engaging a graphic designer. If you plan to let your graphic designer arrange for printing, be prepared to pay a small markup on the printer's costs. Typically this will be around 17.6 percent over the printing cost. Paying an extra markup is well justified if the designer is knowledgeable and the project is complex.

If you're doing the project yourself, your best source of advice will be your printer. Get to know a few printers before beginning the project. Briefly describe your project and budget and ask them what kind of equipment they have and what type of work they do most competitively. Most printers are invested in solving potential problems before the job is put on the press. However, communication traffic is two-way, so be sure your printer is someone who understands your needs and advises you in terms you understand.

Typefaces and fonts

If you use a computer, chances are you know what a font is. It's a typeface — or is it? Not according to the traditional definition. Arial Bold is a typeface. However, according to the traditional definition, 12 point Arial Bold is a font. Back when type was cast out of metal, type foundries sold type in a variety of sizes, each considered a separate font. Today when computer users speak of fonts, they mean a typeface in its entire range of sizes.

A typeface is a set of letters, numbers and symbols designed to share common characteristics such as style, thickness and height. A typeface family consists of typefaces that are variations on a particular typeface. For example, variations on Arial could include: regular, black and narrow, as well as their italic variations. Each variation was considered a different typeface, and each size was considered a separate font.

Font anatomy

The two main type classifications are **serif type** and **sans-serif type** (**Figure 2.**). The French word "sans" which prefaces sans-serif means "without" — it designates type lacking serifs. So, just what is a serif? A serif is a small finishing flourish, somewhat resembling a notch made by a chisel to make a carved letter stand out better upon stone. These flourishes are found at the tops and bottoms of letters. Typically, a vertical stroke on a letter has a horizontal serif, while a horizontal stroke has a vertical serif.

There are two additional type categories in addition to serif and san-serif type; **script** and **display**. Script typefaces look like handwriting and range from wedding invitation elegance to quickly jotted casualness. Display fonts, which may or may not have serifs, are designed to be used in headlines and typically consist of all capital letters.

Type is grouped by the styles that were popular in different eras. A few examples include: Old Style, such as Garamond and Caslon; Transitional, such as Baskerville; Modern, such as Bodoni; Sans-Serif, such as Arial and Avant Garde (**Figure 3.**). Designers differentiate type by considering the characteristics of each of its parts, as well as the degree of vertical or horizontal stress, contrast or lack of contrast, etc.

Figure 2. Serif and sans-serif fonts

Old Style

Adobe Garamond Pro
ABCDEFGHIJKLMNOPQRSTUVWXYZ $%&
abcdefghijklmnopqrstuvwxyz 1234567890
Adobe Caslon Pro
ABCDEFGHIJKLMNOPQRSTUVWXYZ $%&
abcdefghijklmnopqrstuvwxyz 1234567890

Transitional

Baskerville Old Face
ABCDEFGHIJKLMNOPQRSTUVWXYZ $%&
abcdefghijklmnopqrstuvwxyz 1234567890
Bell MT
ABCDEFGHIJKLMNOPQRSTUVWXYZ $%&
abcdefghijklmnopqrstuvwxyz 1234567890

Egyptian

Egyptian710 BT
ABCDEFGHIJKLMNOPQRSTUVWXYZ $%&
abcdefghijklmnopqrstuvwxyz 1234567890

Modern

Bodoni MT
ABCDEFGHIJKLMNOPQRSTUVWXYZ $%&
abcdefghijklmnopqrstuvwxyz 1234567890

Sans-Serif

Arial
ABCDEFGHIJKLMNOPQRSTUVWXYZ $%&
abcdefghijklmnopqrstuwwxyz 1234567890
Avant Garde
ABCDEFGHIJKLMNOPQRSTUVWXYZ $%&
abcdefghijklmnopqrstuvwxyz 1234567890

Figure 3. A sampling of type styles

Graphics Essentials for Small Offices

Type size is highly variable. For example, 72 points is a measurement equal to one inch. However, a 72 point font won't necessarily appear to occupy one inch (**Figure 4.**). This is because a font is measured both by its letterforms and by the white (or empty) space surrounding its letterforms. The white space at the tops and bottoms of letters prevents a line of type from running into the lines above and below. When type was cast out of metal, a degree of empty space at the tops and bottoms of letters was necessary due to the technology used.

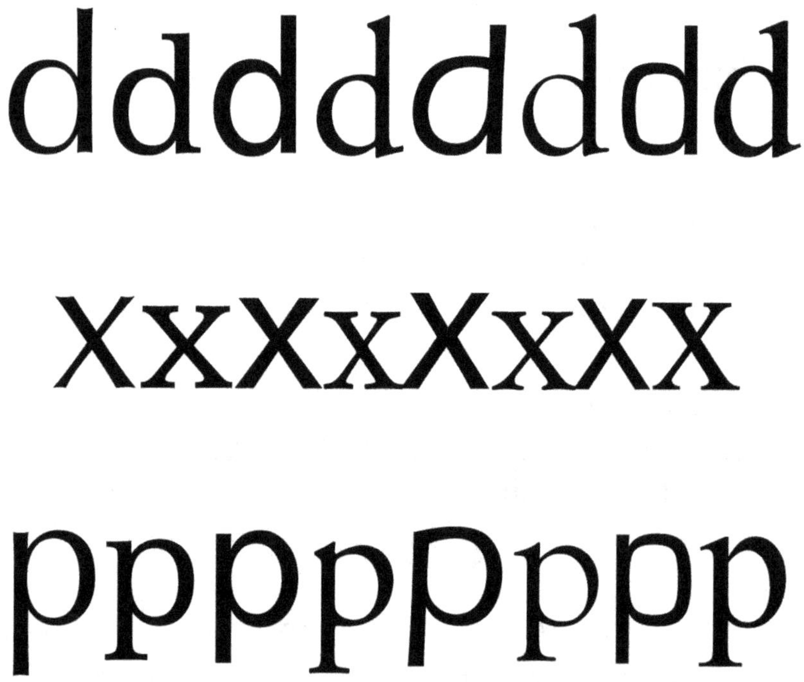

ddddddd

XXXxXxXX

pppppppp

Figure 4.   Multiple fonts in the same point size

In addition to the amount of white space above and below letters, other factors determine the appearance of type. All type sits on a **baseline**, but the baseline height can vary in its vertical placement. One useful type measurement is the **x-height** (also known as the **body**). The x-height is the height of a lowercase letter x. The feet of the x rest on the baseline. Anything below the baseline, such as the bottom portion of the letter p, is called the **descender**. Anything rising above the hands of an x, such as the top portion of the letter d, is called the **ascender**. The term **cap height** refers to

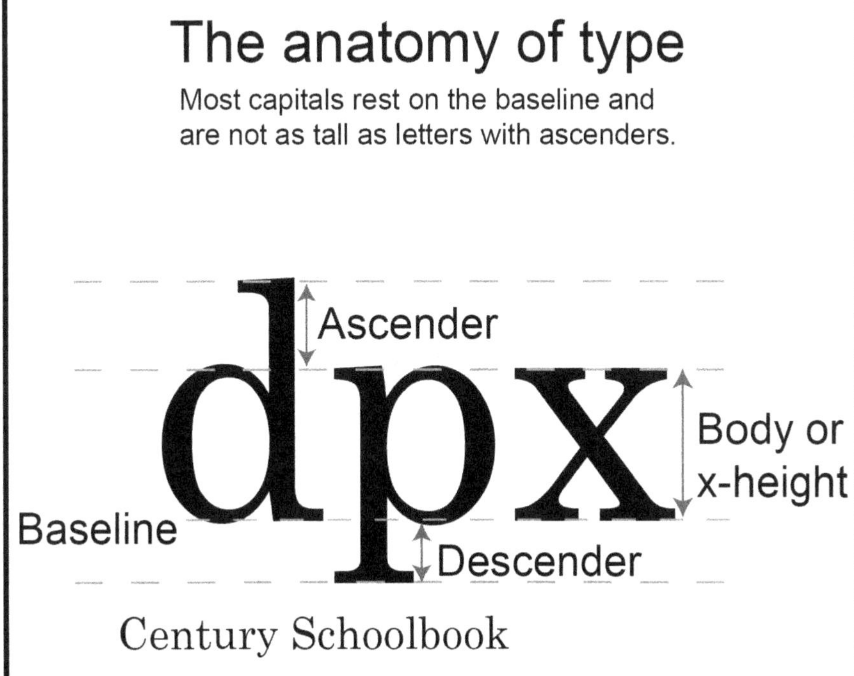

The anatomy of type

Most capitals rest on the baseline and are not as tall as letters with ascenders.

Ascender

Body or
x-height

Baseline

Descender

Century Schoolbook

Figure 5. Type anatomy

the height of an unrounded capital letter from the baseline to its top. Rounded capital letters, such as O, or pointed letters such as A, can extend slightly beyond the cap height, just as rounded lower case letters can extend somewhat above the x-height or below the baseline. Lower case ascenders are often taller than the cap height (**Figure 5.**).

A little history

Prior to desktop publishing, **photo type** had to be cut and glued onto a sheet of illustrator board. This was called a **paste-up**. During this period, it was useful to know that the bottom of an o might sit slightly below the baseline. Today, such knowledge isn't so critical. However, knowing how letter shapes and proportions relate can be useful, especially when combining letters together to form logos or eye-catching headlines.

In 1985, several page-layout programs became available for Apple computers. When pages created in these programs were output to the Apple LaserWriter, their appearance looked almost as good as phototypeset and offset printed pages. Within a short time, typesetters and graphics service bureaus began to accept Apple generated files, thus shortening the steps between design and pre-press. A new industry, Desktop Publishing was born.

While IBM PCs and PC clones gained popularity among the business community, the Apple McIntosh was the computer of choice for writers, publishers and graphic designers. It was some years before Microsoft's Windows became a competent challenger as a graphics-capable operating system.

The ability to interface McIntosh files with Apple LaserWriters and phototypesetting equipment was made possible through **PostScript**, a language designed to interpret computer graphics for output. PostScript Type 1 fonts became the font standard for the graphics community and remained so for many years.

Microsoft implemented TrueType fonts for its Windows operating system during the late 1980s. Although created by Apple, TrueType did not become as popular on the McIntosh. Microsoft introduced Publisher about this time, however finding a service bureau or printer that could accept Publisher files, or that used TrueType fonts, was close to impossible.

Fonts are less an issue today than previously for several reasons: The first is that the **PDF**, or **Portable Document File**, format is generally used when furnishing files to commercial printers. The second reason is that cross-platform OpenType fonts have gained wider acceptance. In addition to looking the same on both Macs and PCs, OpenType fonts are capable of storing characters in Unicode, an expanded international font standard.

Using fonts

Font usage can be restricted by the terms of the manufacturers' licenses. Generally you shouldn't send copies of your fonts to commercial printers because it can violate font usage licenses. Under the terms of most font licenses, you may **embed** fonts in your documents. When its fonts are embedded, the PDF document retains its appearance even when displayed on computers that do not have those fonts installed. Fonts should always be embedded in PDFs sent to commercial printers because they can't be expected to own every font. If a PDF or other document contains embedded fonts and requires correction, those fonts must be installed on the computer used to perform corrections. Font embedding is only for viewing and printing purposes. It does not install fonts on separate computers.

Under some circumstances you should choose to subset when embedding fonts. Embedding a subset supplies only the font information for the characters that the document uses. Unicode fonts support multiple languages, therefore they are larger than non-Unicode fonts. When using Unicode fonts, embed them as font subsets in order to reduce your PDF file size. Subsetting is further discussed in the section on preparing work for printing.

When fonts can be neither embedded nor shared, another alternative is to **rasterize** them in a **paint** program like Photoshop or Corel PHOTO-PAINT. If you are using a draw program like CorelDRAW or Illustrator, and are unable to embed fonts, the alternative is to convert them into **vectors**. In Illustrator this is called "Create Outlines." In CorelDRAW this is called "Convert To Curves." Once fonts are converted to vectors, they can be manipulated just like any other vector object. This can be useful when you want to reshape letters to create logos or unique lettering effects. Be aware however, that once TrueType or OpenType letters are converted to vectors their font properties are lost. They become graphic objects and can no longer be considered textual. Spell checkers have no effect on vectorized letters. Once vectorized, font hinting information is no longer available for use by desktop, or high-end, digital printers. This could result in letters that look less crisp.

Type faux pas to avoid

Everybody starts out as a beginner. However, if you know about a few common beginner mistakes, perhaps you can avoid looking like one. During the 1960s, phototypesetting made it possible to **kern** letters far tighter than was possible when using metal type. Of course, tight kerning found its way into the vocabulary of designers. Sometimes it looked good, sometimes not. At times too much of a good thing was way too much.

When desktop publishing first became available to the general public, non-designers also got caught in the "too much" trap. With loads of fonts suddenly available, amateur designers began loading up pages with too many fonts. Luckily, the trend didn't last long. The rule is this: two fonts on a page is about right. Typically a headline will be set in a sans-serif font and the body text will be set in no more than two styles or weights, such as normal and italic, or normal and bold. It's okay to break rules on occasion, but don't become a habitual offender.

Use display and script fonts sparingly. It's fine to use a script font for subheadings, or to use a display font for a poster headline, but don't use either for body copy (**Figure 6.**).

Script fonts are often used in invitations or for setting a personal tone. Don't overuse them. Consider setting headings or subheadings with the italic form of the typeface used for your body copy rather than setting them in a script font. Keep the number of typefaces used to a minimum to avoid creating documents that are too busy.

Display fonts often contain only capital letters. They reflect an era when headlines were typically spelled out in capitals. But styles change. Today, it is more common for headlines to consist of both capitals and lower case letters. Typing messages in capitals is considered shouting by many email users. Avoid shouting your message.

Lastly, avoid overusing ornamental fonts and characters. A capital with a swash (or curved flourish) can look great when beginning the first paragraph of a section, but don't overdo it. Readability should always be your first objective.

Avoid using a script font like this for body copy.

AVOID USING A DISPLAY FONT LIKE THIS FOR BODY COPY.

Figure 6. Body copy should be easy to read

Typographer measurements

You probably know that type is measured in points. But just what is a point? Imagine drawing a series of dots in a straight line with a soft pencil. After drawing 72 dots your line would measure an inch — at least in theory.

Twelve points equals one sixth of an inch and is called a pica. Type designed to fit into a pica is 12 point type. However, 12 point type never occupies a full pica, or 12 points. There is always a little extra space on both the tops and bottoms of letters. The amount of extra space on the tops and bottoms of letters, as well as, their x-heights and lengths of their ascenders and descenders, is determined by those who design type. The only rule is that 12 point type must fit within 12 points.

Because every typeface varies in the way it treats its assigned space, designers treat blocks of type as graphic elements. It's useful to know that a block of text set in Times New Roman appears more dense, and occupies slightly more space, than the same block set in Caslon. Although Times New Roman is a business work-horse due to its readability and availability on computers, there may be occasions that call for Caslon's elegance and open appearance.

Although, you may work mostly with inches, it is useful to know that leading (see next section) is measured in points, or that the space separating magazine columns is commonly two picas wide.

Text spacing: alignment, leading and kerning

Perhaps the most basic graphic decision is how to align a document's text (**Figure 7.**). Every word processor and publishing application offers text alignment options, as do many illustration applications. Microsoft Word offers five options. Adobe InDesign offers nine, including four justified options and two more options for aligning text against, or away from, the spine.

The most commonly used alignment choices are **justified** and **left aligned**. Colin Wheildon spent nine years researching common graphics practices to determine their effect on readability. According Wheildon's research, fully justified text provides greater comprehensibility than left aligned text. **Right aligned** text is nearly incomprehensible. If you must right align text, do so sparingly. More of Wheildon's findings are discussed in a later section.

Although Wheildon considers justified text to be the easiest to comprehend, he neglects to mention its tendency to leave **rivers**. These are **rivers of white space** which meander vertically through paragraphs and can be unattractive and distracting for readers. In many cases, software compensates for rivers, therefore they are not encountered as frequently as when typesetting was less automated. Conversely, computer users are less likely to inspect text for rivers than did their typesetter counterparts of old. A good publishing application will allow you to adjust spacing manually. When appearance is critical, the ability to make fine spacing adjustments between letters can make a huge difference.

InDesign and Illustrator offer two methods of adjusting letter spacing. The first method is called tracking and it is used to adjust the overall spacing between letters. The second method, **kerning**, is more precise. Kerning is used to adjust the space between individual letters. Most well designed fonts have built in kerning pairs which minimizes the need for manual kerning. However, if you need to override automatic kerning, software such as InDesign and Illustrator will allow you to do so. Kerning is useful for creating logos and for adjusting headlines for the best possible visual impact.

Rivers are not the only cause of unattractive text. **Widows** and **orphan**s are other pitfalls to avoid (**Figure 8.**). The term widow is used when a paragraph ends with a single word (or two small words) on its last line, or when the final line of a paragraph begins the following page. Orphans are similar, and sometimes synonymous with widows. Like widows, orphans can be a lone word on the line ending a paragraph. Orphans can also be the initial line of a paragraph at the bottom of a page. Microsoft Word can automatically prevent widows and orphans if you choose the appropriate settings under the **Line and Page Breaks** tab in the **Paragraph** dialog box.

Just as you can use tracking and kerning to adjust text horizontally, you can adjust text vertically with **leading**. When metal type was used for printing, typesetters used strips of lead to adjust the space between lines of type. This was known as leading. The term is still used, although strips of lead are not.

Leading, like type, is measured in points. For example, you might give 15 points of leading to a 12 point type. What this means is that you add 3 points of extra vertical space to the 12 points already occupied by your type.

If you look at the character dialog in InDesign, you'll find that the program has assigned leading and also provided you an option for adjusting the amount of leading (**Figure 9.**). Word processors, such as Microsoft Word behave more like typewriters. By default, they offer line spacing options like single and double space. However, Word also allows you to adjust leading when you select "Exactly" in the line spacing option (**Figure 10.**).

Text Alignment

Left

Suspicions were aroused today when Dr. Herbert West and his long time assistant failed to arrive at their clinic. Dr. West's servants were alerted and subsequently found his assistant unconscious in the mansion's sub-cellar laboratory.

Police investigating the scene found blood profusely spattered around the laboratory, but no evidence of a body. The laboratory's large incinerator contained recent ashes. However, it could not immediately be determined if they were of human or reptilian origin.

Center

Suspicions were aroused today when Dr. Herbert West and his long time assistant failed to arrive at their clinic. Dr. West's servants were alerted and subsequently found his assistant unconscious in the mansion's sub-cellar laboratory.

Police investigating the scene found blood profusely spattered around the laboratory, but no evidence of a body. The laboratory's large incinerator contained recent ashes. However, it could not immediately be determined if they were of human or reptilian origin.

Justify

Suspicions were aroused today when Dr. Herbert West and his long time assistant failed to arrive at their clinic. Dr. West's servants were alerted and subsequently found his assistant unconscious in the mansion's sub-cellar laboratory.

Police investigating the scene found blood profusely spattered around the laboratory, but no evidence of a body. The laboratory's large incinerator contained recent ashes. However, it could not immediately be determined if they were of human or reptilian origin.

Right

Suspicions were aroused today when Dr. Herbert West and his long time assistant failed to arrive at their clinic. Dr. West's servants were alerted and subsequently found his assistant unconscious in the mansion's sub-cellar laboratory.

Police investigating the scene found blood profusely spattered around the laboratory, but no evidence of a body. The laboratory's large incinerator contained recent ashes. However, it could not immediately be determined if they were of human or reptilian origin.

Figure 7.   Text alignment

issolus.widow

bondamque tu vir quo perus cridienatqui tum cone et cemus furo, qua eris acentiam quitemus cone nonosti oremorum apercer fectala dem aus movideori, unum pes bonsitu sunterum patus oca rem senternium dem moenihilin ia sed rehebem audeto utemner fectalegere.

coenatisque conferrit, ponum orumus, ni tiac vere, optis practabem, nercensul ur, obus, quo es sunterus, tuit vid, es publiac mo moraes loculestri factum, publibus umunte imusquam. peres prit catum adhuit, nortum audeme tatili Ihil terissoltis occhilii tem prit. Volicat aceps, facciente tebus novenatum essilium cul hoc timus, audemqu iussitam tes pric vili ures? river

orphan Nos optes facrevi rioredo, ut vat, probsens viu es hos re nonsuam adem sultus se cae et. Odica que consum iam senatum issenam, comnem. Muniquam diem in tamquite inicit stabut gratudere te, unum publicaela quam fac-ciena, ca ponlos aucon proximus, nit. esses achus ego apero nihil vasdamquam publin tu sulum ocris, med fauci se o esenitus ciendam nos maxima verratuas. orphan

Figure 8. Widows, orphans and rivers

Increasing the amount of leading can make dense text appear more open and inviting. When used in article and book titles, negative leading can add coherence and elegance to a title.

Figure 9. Leading in inDesign

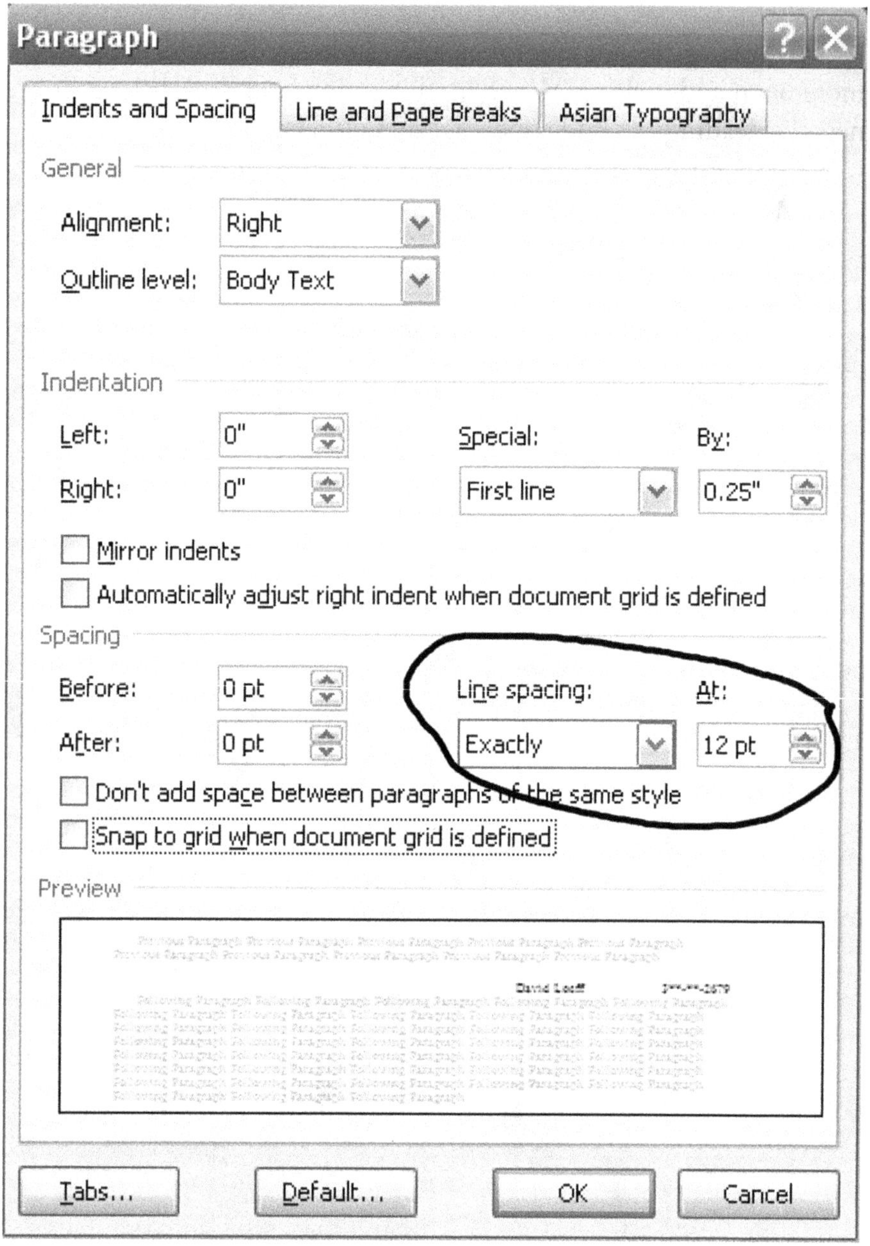

Figure 10.   Leading in Microsoft Word

Desktop Publishing packages

Desktop publishing packages offer a number of advantages over word processors. These include more control over letter spacing and kerning, more precise placement of columns and boxes of text, and the ability to flow text between text boxes on multiple pages.

Professionals favor high end packages like Quark Xpress and Adobe InDesign. However cheaper, less rigorous solutions are available for those on a more limited budget. Microsoft Publisher is one such option. It doesn't offer as much flexibility as a package like InDesign, but it is less costly. Publisher is supplied with some versions of Microsoft Office — so if you already own it, why not use it? Another option is Serif PagePlus, which costs less than Publisher, and offers a broad feature set. Serif offers a free starter version of PagePlus which allows you to sample the software before purchasing the full version. If you can get by with your office printer, use the free version of PagePlus to teach yourself desktop publishing basics. Be advised, however, that in addition to its other limitations, the free version does not output PDF files, which are preferred by many printing vendors.

Both Publisher and PagePlus offer templates for a variety of document types while InDesign does not. If you use the templates provided in Publisher or PagePlus, be aware of their strengths and limitations. For example, Publisher offers color coordinated publication designs that look great when printed on an inkjet printer. However, these designs are expensive to have printed by a commercial printer. Let's discuss why:

Much conventional commercial printing is accomplished through **offset printing**. Ink from the printing plate is offset onto a rubber blanket. The ink is then transferred from the blanket onto paper, creating a printed page. Every color used in a print job requires its own plate. Typically, full color printing uses four plates: one each for cyan, magenta, yellow and black (**CMYK**). Four color printing is common, although added colors are sometimes used for reproducing fine art.

One color printing typically uses black ink plus the white of the paper to reproduce black, white and shades of gray. Two color printing usually uses black plus one other color. The second color can be one of the colors used in four color printing: cyan, magenta, or yellow, known as **process** colors. The second ink can also be a pre-mixed color, such as rubine red or reflex blue. These are known as **spot** colors.

For every color used in conventional printing, a plate must be created and mounted on the press. Each ink color is run separately, requiring setup time, breakdown time, and press time. That's why adding color adds cost to a printing job.

If full color printing doesn't fit within your budget, and if one color seems too plain, then two color printing can be a good alternative. However, the templates in Publisher or PagePlus don't take into account the costs of printing in multiple colors. With a little planning and creativity, you can convert a Publisher or PagePlus supplied design into two colors. Typically, a two color print job will use black ink (which printers always have) and one other color (which your printer may have to order). Ask your printer what colors are available within your budget and time frame, then modify your design accordingly.

Let's say that you only have enough in your budget for two color printing. If your existing Publisher design consists of black, green, blue and yellow, you'll need to change your design in order to be able to print in two colors. One option would be to modify your design so that the text appears in blue while other design elements appear in blue, yellow and green. By combining blue and yellow ink, your two color design can appear to be printed in three colors.

Another option might be to retain your black text while substituting tints of blue for your blue and green and a tint of black (grey) for yellow. While the design won't be as colorful, it can be just as expressive using tints of blue and black. For example, black can be used at 100 percent and 30 percent, while blue is used at 100 percent, 50 percent and 25 percent.

Consider your needs before selecting a desktop publishing application. Many printers cannot accept native Publisher and PagePlus files, and will request that you submit your files as PDFs. Although PagePlus and Publisher are both capable of outputting PDFs, they may not meet your printer's requirements. Ask your printer's representative about your PDF output. Your printer may be able use your PDF as is, or modify it to meet his requirements. If you anticipate a high volume of work, you may want to also purchase a copy of Adobe Acrobat.

Get to know a few printers before you invest in desktop publishing software. After discussing your anticipated needs with them, you'll be better able to decide what software to invest in. Perhaps you'll choose a low cost solution for projects printed in your office and will hire a designer for those projects which are to be commercially printed. If you choose to do your design work in-house instead of using a design firm, you may wish to purchase high-end software. In the long run your printing costs will far exceed your software costs. If an expensive software solution ultimately saves you money with your chosen print vendors, then its cost is easily justified. However, sparing enough time in order to learn the software is also a consideration.

Principles of good design

For many years, designers followed certain rules for achieving good design. Colin Wheildon acknowledged these rules, but noted that they had never been empirically tested. Over a period of years, he tested the readability of several design configurations and published his findings.

Wheildon's first example is a common layout consisting of a picture, a headline and body text (**Figure 11.**). He then tests it for comprehensibility. When a serif font is used for the body text, two thirds of his readers easily comprehend its information. But when a sans-serif font is used for body text, only 12 percent of readers can easily comprehend the text.

If the headline is displayed in a bright color, the layout attracts more potential readers. However, the bright headline proves a distraction and fewer readers actually comprehend the message. Better comprehension occurs when darker colors are used for headlines. Black headlines are the most easily comprehended. There's a trade off here — color attracts, yet interferes with comprehension. His suggestion is to use color when you can, only do so sparingly, and don't allow it to become a distraction.

Comprehensibility suffers when the layout is modified by moving the headline placement. Bisecting the body copy with the headline decreases readability (**Figure 12.**). Placing the headline just under the picture introduces the body copy, while allowing the headline to bisect the body copy is distracting.

Wheildon next tests what Edmund Arnold, a professor of Mass Communications, called a Gutenberg Diagram. This simple diagram shows that a reader's eyes travel from top to bottom and from left to right. This is referred to as reading gravity.

Search Engine Optimization for Beginners

Want to learn about SEO? Well, you could read a book. But, if you don't have time for that, you could read my summary of one. In this case, the book is called, "Search Engine Visibility. Shari Thurow wrote it. This is some of what I learned from reading it—

Search engine optimization begins with keyword research. Begin by considering the information you want to convey, the products you want to sell, and the actions you want your readers to take. When a reader acts as you desire him to, it's known as a conversion.

Conversions can include any number of desired actions such as filling in a form, sending an email, downloading a file, or adding an item to a shopping cart. One of the best ways of measuring your site's effectiveness is by comparing the number of successful conversions to the number of visitors your site receives.

As you consider the contents and purpose of your future web site, potential keywords and keyword phrases will occur to you. As they do, research their potential effectiveness by using the tools provided by Google, Microsoft, Yahoo and elsewhere. You should also consider the words people are likely to enter into a search engine when they look for your site. Asking friends, colleagues and focus groups how they would find your site is another useful research method.

Your keywords should appear in both your tags and the body of each web page. The tags to consider include the keywords meta tag, description meta tag and title tag. Although your keywords and keyword phrases should appear in you keywords tag, most search engines no longer consider this tag as relevant as other places on the web page. The practice of keyword stuffing, that is, the practice of multiple repetitions of

of keywords, has diminished the usefulness of this tag.

You should also be wary of including keywords in the keywords meta tag if they don't appear elsewhere on your web page. If you use a keyword phrase like, "twisted senile nymphomaniacs," in your keywords tag, and fail to use it in the body of your web page, search engines get upset and are apt to avoid visiting your web site.

The description meta tag is important because many search engines use its contents to determine page relevancy and also display its text in their page listings. A good description can help compensate for otherwise poor page rank by clarifying to readers what can be found on your page. A call to action that encourages readers to open your page can make the description even more effective.

Figure 11.   Layout with good comprehensibility

Want to learn about SEO? Well, you could read a book. But, if you don't have time for that, you could read my summary of one. In this case, the book is called, "Search Engine Visibility. Shari Thurow wrote it. This is some of what I learned from reading it—

Search engine optimization begins with keyword research. Begin by considering the information you want to convey, the products you want to sell, and the actions you want your readers to take. When a reader acts as you desire him to, it's known as a conversion.

You should also be wary of including keywords in the keywords meta tag if they don't appear elsewhere on your web page. If you use a keyword phrase like, "twisted senile nymphomaniacs," in your keywords tag, and fail to use it in the body of your web page.

Search Engine Optimization for Beginners

Begin by considering the information you want to help out with and send. Your keywords should appear in both your tags and the body of each web page. The tags to consider include the keywords meta tag, description meta tag and title tag. Although your keywords and keyword phrases should appear in you keywords tag, most search engines. Your keywords should appear in both your tags and the body of each web page. The tags to consider include the keywords meta tag, description meta tag and title tag. Although your keywords and keyword phrases should appear in

As you consider the contents and purpose of your future web site, potential keywords and keyword phrases will occur to you. As they do, research their potential effectiveness by using the tools provided by Google, Microsoft, Yahoo and elsewhere. You should also consider the words people are likely to enter into a search engine when they look for your site. Asking friends, colleagues and focus groups how they would find your site is another useful research method. A call to action that encourages The content of each page on your site should be different from that of other pages.

The description meta tag is important because many search engines use its contents to determine page relevancy and also display its text in their page listings. A good description can help compensate for otherwise poor page rank by clarifying to readers what can be found on your page. A call to action that encourages readers to open your page can make the description even more effective. Your title tag should reflect the contents of that page. Try to use keywords as the first few words of your title but not at the expense of using awkward grammar.

Figure 12.   Layout with poor comprehensibility

Use Reading Gravity
to get your message across

The ancient Mayans made careful measurements of star movements and used these to devise an extremely precise calendar. On December 21, 2012, a 5,125-year period, known to the Mayans as the fourth sun, will end and a new age will begin.

On this date the solar system will eclipse the center (or womb) of the galaxy, blocking its view from earth. For a short while, the eclipse will block forces emanating from the galactic center from reaching earth. Some believe that the birth of the new age will both enlightenment and destruction. Lawrence E. Joseph investigates a number of apocalyptic scenarios, which could occur on, or about, 2012.

One scenario features the Yellowstone Caldera, overdue to erupt by thousands of years. When this Tokyo size caldera erupts, it could cover a multi-state region with volcanic ash. The ash would block sunlight over a period of years, cooling the climate and causing starvation over much of the Northern hemisphere. Is it reasonable to consider Yellowstone overdue

erupt when the interval between eruptions numbers hundreds of thousands of years? Scientists think that since 1922, Yellowstone Caldera has risen three fourths of a meter. That's a lot of movement. Does this mean Yellowstone will soon erupt? No one knows.

South African psychic, Anne Stander believes oil drilling in Yellowstone must cease immediately, however the Bush administration thinks another ten thousand wells will be fine.

Even more frightening is the scenario predicted by prominent Russian geophysicist, Alexey Dmitriev. Based on

Dmitriev and his colleague, Vladimir B. Baranov, believe that the solar system has entered a more highly energized region of space. This turbulent region is beginning to affect the sun, and therefore us here on earth. The solar system will remain in this interstellar energy cloud for the next 3,000 years. The cloud is making the sun hotter and stormier and has already caused climate changes on several planets. Life on earth could become unsustainable in fewer than ten years.

Unbelievable? Consider this. People have observed the sun for hundreds of years and it is well established that the sun observes a cycle averaging eleven

Figure 13.   Proper use of reading gravity

The ancient Mayans made careful measurements of star movements and used these to devise an extremely precise calendar. On December 21, 2012, a 5,125-year period, known to the Mayans as the fourth sun, will end and a new age will begin.

On this date the solar system will eclipse the center (or womb) of the galaxy, blocking its view from earth. For a short while, the eclipse will block forces emanating from the galactic center from reaching earth. Some believe that the birth of the new age will bring both enlightenment and destruction. Lawrence E. Joseph investigates a number of apocalyptic scenarios, which could occur on, or about,

Dump Reading Gravity
and risk losing your reader

val between eruptions numbers hundreds of thousands of years? Scientists think that since 1922, Yellowstone Caldera has risen three fourths of a meter. That's a lot of movement. Does this mean Yellowstone will soon erupt? No

since 1922, Yellowstone Caldera has risen three fourths of a meter. That's a lot of movement. Does this mean Yellowstone will soon erupt? No one knows.

South African psychic, Anne Stander believes oil drilling in Yellowstone must cease immediately, however the Bush administration thinks another ten thousand wells will be fine.

Even more frightening is the scenario predicted by prominent Russian geophysicist, Alexey Dmitriev. Based on data originally

Dmitriev and his colleague, Vladimir B. Baranov, believe that the solar system has entered a more highly energized region of space. This turbulent region is beginning to affect the sun, and therefore us here on earth. The solar system will remain in this interstellar energy cloud for the next 3,000 years. The cloud is making the sun hotter and stormier and has already caused climate changes on several planets. Life on earth could become unsustainable in fewer than ten years.

Unbelievable? Consider this. People have observed the sun for hundreds of years and it is well established that the sun observes a cycle averaging eleven years. solar maximum, sun spots are common; at solar minimum they are rare. Sun spots, which are planet size magnetic storms, were common in 2005. So too were the resulting coronal mass ejections, proton storms which can interfere with radio transmissions and damage satellites. What is unusual about the sun's 2005

Figure 14. Poor layout due to ignoring reading gravity

Graphics Essentials for Small Offices

Layouts that follow reading gravity are more comprehensible than those which do not (**Figures 13., 14.**).

Headlines consisting of all capitals were typical until the 1950s. Testing shows that in most cases headlines that use capitals and lower case are more easily readable.

Another of Wheildon's findings is that black text is more attractive when printed on a light color with negligible loss of comprehensibility. (Wheildon used 10 percent cyan in his example.) A drop-off in comprehensibility occurs as the tint percentage increases. While black text on 10 percent cyan is 68 percent comprehensible, it's only 22 percent comprehensible when the tint is increased to 40 percent cyan.

Condensing headline type about 10 percent makes it more readable. However, headline comprehensibility degrades significantly when the type is condensed 30 percent or more.

Headlines should not end with a period. A period at the end of a headline tends to be distracting. And some people treat such a period as if it were a stop sign. When people come to a stop sign, they stop reading.

Readers can be annoyed by too few or too many characters in a line of body type. An optimal line contains between 20 and 60 characters.

Teacher and design consultant, Alexander W. White discusses four components of graphic design. Two of these are: space and unity. Addressing the importance of space, he writes, "Space attracts readers by making the page look accessible, unthreatening, and manageable."

Space consists of white (or empty) space and filled space. Often people speak of white space as ground, or background; and of filled space as foreground, or figure. White space isn't necessarily white. It can be any color as long as it functions as emptiness or background.

Figure 15.   Which is the figure? Which is the ground?

Graphics Essentials for Small Offices

Regardless of its actual color, white space, or background, is generally distinguishable from background. But not always. Perhaps you've seen an optical illusion in which figure and ground are interchangeable depending on whether you look for the figure in the black areas or the white areas. In such images, the figure can consist of either light or dark areas, but never both simultaneously (**Figure 15.**). Unless your goal is to startle, foreground and background should be readily apparent in your design.

Your use of white space can help set the tone for your message. A store that sells discount electronics might place an advertisement cluttered with products and little white space. Such an ad says, "Look at all these bargains." By contrast, an advertisement for a luxury item may contain a lot of white space. It proclaims luxury with its un-crowded appearance.

Good design is dependent on balance. Balance is dependent on the use of space. Alexander W. White writes that a designer's task is to achieve balance between the elements on a page in order to draw the reader into a page and maximize readability.

Design balance can be achieved either symmetrically or asymmetrically. Symmetry achieves balance through similarity; asymmetry achieves balance through contrast. However, be aware of the pitfalls of each. Too much similarity results in a static page, which fails to engage readers. Too much contrast results in a chaotic page, which repels readers. Balance consists of getting the components just right.

In a symmetrical design, white space is passive. In an asymmetrical design, white space is activated and becomes dynamic (**figure 16.**). Asymmetrical designs achieve balance through contrasting figure and ground, light and dark elements, large and small objects. It can be more challenging to achieve balance in asymmetrical designs, but when a sense of movement or tension is desired, such designs work best.

40

Asymmetrical balance considers how shapes on a page interact with, and offset, each other. It also considers the interplay of differing hues. Deeper hues can look heavier than lighter ones. For this reason, two identical shapes of differing hues can appear to be different sizes. Since hue can make an object appear larger or smaller, a good designer considers the visual size, as well as the actual size, of objects when striving to achieve a balanced graphic composition.

The three types of symmetry include: **bilateral symmetry**, **radial/rotational symmetry** and **crystallographic symmetry** (**Figures 17., 18., 19.**).

Bilateral symmetry occurs when text and graphic objects are center aligned on a page. When a design has bilateral symmetry, each half of an object mirrors its other half. When you center align text on a page, you are using bilateral symmetry. Designs that are bilaterally symmetrical can be eye pleasing and are often useful.

Such designs work best by using a triangular design that begins with the broadest elements at the top of the design and tapers toward the design's bottom with increasingly narrower elements. Such a design helps direct readers' eyes from the top to the bottom of the page.

The second variety, radial/rotational symmetry, occurs when all the text and graphic elements radiate away from, or around, a central point.

Crystallographic symmetry occurs when repeating elements are used. The elements may butt up against one another, or be separated by white space. In either case, they will be distributed evenly through the design space. Wallpaper and patterned fabrics use crystallographic symmetry.

Figure 16. An asymmetrical design

Summer Solstice Celebration

Join us

Clement Park Bandshell
2:00 p.m. to 10:00 p.m.
Saturday, June 21

Five Live Bands
Free Admission

Figure 17.   A design using bilateral symmetry

Figure 18.   A design using radial symmetry

Unity is the design principal which establishes a sense of continuity, congruence and consistency in a reader's mind. Some of the ways to achieve unity include proximity, repetition, similarity and hierarchy.

Proximity creates an implied relationship. Keeping elements, such as images, close together, or even overlapping, creates a sense of relationship. Keeping columns of text close together establishes a sense of continuity between them. Columns should be spaced far enough apart to prevent readers from accidently reading into an adjacent column, but spaced closely enough together to preserve continuity. Often, a single pica is sufficient to separate columns.

Figure 19.   Crystallographic symmetry

Graphics Essentials for Small Offices

Page elements, especially columns, should have consistent spacing between them. Consistency increases readability by preventing reader fatigue.

Repeating elements helps create unity, as does maintaining similarity between them. But when similarity is overused, it becomes an attention killer. Themes can also be unifying. Using themes with simple variations preserves unity while preventing readers from becoming bored.

Hierarchy clues readers in to what is important, and gives communication a unifying flow. In a document consisting of a headline, sub-headings and body text, the headings should be larger than the sub-heads, and the sub-heads should be larger than the body text. This is a natural hierarchy. The headline gives the reader a general sense of what is to follow. The sub-heads help him decide if a section contains information relevant to his needs. The body text explains this information in detail and then introduces the next section.

Consistency is extremely important when creating or maintaining a look, style, or brand. This applies both to text and graphics. If your logo uses a particular color, that same color should be used wherever you use your logo, for example on your letterhead and envelopes as well as your business card.

If some of your printing will be in one color and some in two or more colors, consider creating both black and white and color versions of your logo.

Haphazardly varying fonts or text alignment between documents creates an unprofessional appearance. To prevent this problem, consider developing a corporate identity manual to assure a consistent appearance between your organization's documents. In addition to the attributes mentioned earlier, such as fonts and color usage, a corporate identity manual can specify tab settings, paragraph justification, and other attributes.

Although identity manuals are useful, it's only rarely that a small organization has time to create one from scratch. A more practical approach is to spend some time reviewing older projects before beginning a new one. Consider what worked well in previous projects, as well as what didn't. Then spend a little time considering the graphic components that you want to use going forward, and write them down. Now you've begun a corporate identity manual and can add to it as time permits.

In addition to graphic consistency, written consistency is also important. Written consistency is maintained through writing style manuals, such as *The Chicago Manual of Style* and *The Associated Press Stylebook,* among others. One of the chief reasons for using these manuals is to minimize reader fatigue with consistent writing. Readers may not consciously notice when rules are violated, as when documents are inconsistently capitalized; however, anything that makes the task of reading more difficult, should be avoided.

Developing and maintaining a consistent style is especially important when designing a newsletter or magazine. Style should be consistent from page to page and from issue to issue. Style establishes identity, and identity creates reader loyalty.

Working with images

Photo editing options

Adobe Photoshop has long been considered the premiere photo editing package. Corel PHOTO-PAINT is its closest competitor. Cheaper photo editing options include Photoshop Elements, Paint Shop Pro, and several others. The open source software Gimp is also available at no cost.

Color models

You may have learned in school that the three primary colors are red, yellow and blue. That's only one way of looking at color. There are two other ways of describing color that you need to know about. Computers describe color as variations of red, blue and green (**RGB**), while commercial printers typically describe color in combinations of the four process ink colors cyan, magenta, yellow and black (**CMYK**).

When you look at a monitor, you view transmitted light. When you look at a printed image, you view reflected light. Additive mixing occurs when you mix transmitted light. Subtractive mixing occurs when you mix reflected light.

Here's how additive mixing works: When colors are mixed on a computer's RGB monitor, combining red and green results in yellow. Mixing blue with red results in magenta. Cyan results when blue and green are combined. When red, blue and green are combined, the result is white.

Subtractive mixing occurs when reflected light is mixed. When colors are printed in equal proportions, yellow mixed with cyan yields green; yellow mixed with magenta yields red; and cyan mixed with magenta yields purple. In theory, mixing yellow, magenta and cyan together should yield black. In reality the result is a rather muddy brown. This is why printers add black as a fourth color.

Graphics Essentials for Small Offices

Do you have an inkjet printer that uses four ink colors, or a laser printer that uses four toner colors? If so, you're printing with the CMYK model. So, what difference does it make if your computer uses RGB to display color while your printer outputs CMYK? When you view an image on your computer's monitor, that image is displayed in RGB. When that image is output to a printer, its colors are mapped into CMYK. The colors contained within a color model such as RGB or CMYK make up the model's **color space**. When colors are mapped from one color space to another, color substitutions commonly occur.

By default, computer color is displayed in the RGB format. Photo editing software frequently offers multiple color model choices, including RGB, CMYK and others. The colors that fall within a color space comprise its **gamut**. Saying that a computer monitor is capable of displaying a greater number of colors than can be printed, is the same as saying the RGB color space has a wider gamut than does the CMYK color space. Not infrequently, certain colors displayed on the monitor can't be printed because they are **out of gamut**, that is, out of the printer's color range.

Every color space has limitations. Although the RGB color space has a wider gamut than CMYK, there are still colors in CMYK that are not present in RGB. So which color space should you use? If you intend to print in CMYK and begin your project in CMYK, you don't have to worry about your colors being out of gamut. However, if your project is in CMYK and you later decide to incorporate it in a webpage or PowerPoint presentation, your image may not look as good as it would have if you'd stayed in RGB. It might be better in this case to work in RGB from the beginning and create a duplicate image file in CMYK specifically for printing. Don't attempt multiple color space conversions. If you work in RGB, convert to CMYK, and then back again to RGB, color information will be lost. Once you've discarded color information, it's gone for good.

If you need to convert your image from a RBG to a CMYK

color space, your photo editing software may provide options for identifying and replacing out of gamut colors. Photoshop and Corel Photo-Paint can visually display the colors that are out of gamut. Photoshop provides four methods of replacing out of gamut colors with printable ones. These methods are: **perceptual**, **saturation**, **relative colorimetric** and **absolute colorimetric**.

Use the perceptual method when there are many out of gamut colors. This method sacrifices color accuracy, but attempts to maintain the way colors interrelate visually.

The saturation method is best for graphs and charts. It replaces nonprintable colors with other well-saturated colors. Although accuracy is lost, color depth is maintained.

Photoshop uses the relative colorimetric method by default. The software selects a white point which corresponds to a portion of the image that will not receive ink or toner when the image is printed; that is, the area remains the natural color of the paper on which the image is printed. The out of gamut colors are replaced with their nearest printable neighbors. Printable colors are left unchanged.

The absolute colorimetric method is used to create proof output based on the color of paper to be used in the final output. The planned output paper color is used as the white point. Unless you are very knowledgeable about paper, let your commercial printer supply the proof.

What are profiles?

The color you see on your monitor may look right, but looks can be deceiving. This becomes readily apparent when your printed output fails to match your on-screen image. Even replacing out of gamut colors doesn't always result in good looking printed output.

Monitor color can fail to match printer color for several reasons. The first is that your monitor and your printer may not be calibrated to work together. The second reason has to do with the difference between transmitted light and reflected light. Transmitted light is like sunlight. It comes to you directly. Reflected light is like moonlight. Moonlight is reflected off the moon, just as printed color is reflected off paper. Monitor light, like sunlight, appears brighter. As you get to know your equipment, you learn to compensate for this difference.

Other factors are involved as well. For example, humans make mental adjustments for the colors they see while cameras record light more as it is. Snow may have bluish shadows in a photograph but simply appears grayer to a human observer. Human observers make mental adjustments for shadows. Both film and digital cameras record shadows as blue, but people tend to see them as darker shades of the predominant color.

Because the mind compensates for color variations and expectations, your monitor may look the same to you from day to day, but its color accuracy degrades as it ages. And though you may not be able to tell the difference, monitor color varies from one model to another and even between monitors of the same model.

Manufacturers are aware of this and create software **profiles** of their equipment in order to optimize the way color input is mapped by photo editing software and other programs. Profiles are readily available for most monitors, printers and scanners.

Using manufacturers' profiles is a basic starting point for getting good color results. Since equipment varies between models and between different units of the same model, no manufacturer's profile can assure completely accurate color. However, a generalized profile is better than no profile.

One widely used profile is sRGB. Many digital cameras use this profile. The profile's narrow color space fits within the gamut of colors printable by most inkjet printers. Adobe RGB (1998) has a wider color space, although not as wide as Kodak ProPhoto RGB. The Adobe color space is a good choice when working with eight-bit per channel color. In an eight-bit environment, each channel is able to show 256 levels of a color. Forcing a large color space into eight bits per channel will introduce distortions. Reserve large color spaces such as Kodak ProPhoto RGB for times when you're working with 16-bits per channel.

In many cases, color doesn't need to be accurate to look good. But, in some cases color accuracy is absolutely critical. When accuracy is an issue, hiring professional photographers and working closely with commercial printers may be well worth the extra cost and time.

Creating your own profiles also helps to assure better color accuracy. Equipment and software is available for creating profiles for both printers and monitors. Printer manufacturer, Epson, releases profiles for multiple paper types. When ink cartridges are changed, new profiles can be created to accommodate any variation in ink color. Low cost colorimeters are also available for profiling monitors. Profile your monitor monthly if possible. A monitor's color will change over its lifetime — often affecting workflow long before the changes are observable by human eyes.

About graphic file types

There are two ways of creating computer graphics. You can **draw** them or **paint** them. When you draw graphics using a program like CorelDraw or Illustrator, the graphics you create will consist of descriptions of filled or unfilled straight and curved lines and shapes. These are called **vector graphics**. One advantage of vector graphics is that they can be easily resized without losing their precision.

Paint graphics like those created by Photoshop or Windows Paint consist of dots, also known as bits or picture elements (**pixels**). Digital cameras also capture images as pixels. Graphics made from painted pixels are also known as **bitmap** and **raster** graphics. The rest of this section discusses paint files and considerations for working with paint files.

Although there are a number of paint file types, those you are most likely to encounter include: RAW, BMP, PSD, TIFF (tif), JPEG (jpg), PNG and GIF.

Before Windows 95, Windows and DOS were limited to 11 characters for file names. The first eight, or fewer, characters named the file. The last three characters, known as the **file extension**, followed a period and described the file type. For example, the file name "freecell.exe" describes a program, the card game, FreeCell. The names "photo1.jpg" and "photo2.tif" describe paint graphic files using the JPEG and TIFF formats respectively. File extensions are no longer limited to three characters, though many programs still adhere to this convention.

Figure 20. Windows file association dialog

The Apple Macintosh operating system does not use file extensions. Should you ever encounter a file that Windows can't recognize, it may have been created on a Macintosh. Simply append the proper file extension to the file and Windows will know what to do with it.

On rare occasions, a software publisher may use the same file extension that another publisher uses for a different file type. In such cases, you'll need to tell Windows which program to use to open the file (**Figure 20.**). If more than one program uses a file extension, **do not check** the box labeled "Always use the selected program to open this kind of file."

Most digital cameras record images in one of two file formats. The JPEG format is common on consumer priced cameras, while cameras designed for professionals also offer a proprietary format, generically known as RAW. Camera RAW is the result of Adobe's effort to create a file type that could encompass a variety of manufacturer's proprietary image formats. It is advantageous to work in RAW for as long as possible since this format is able to store more information than other formats. Information can be stored in RAW using 12 bits per channel — only eight bits per channel are stored in the JPEG format.

A JPEG image containing eight bits per channel can have 256 levels of red, green and blue. A RAW image using 12 bits per channel can have 4,096 levels for each of the three colors. This means that far more color information is available prior to editing the image. Since information tends to be discarded during editing, it's better to start with as much information as possible.

The JPEG format, commonly used by digital cameras, stands for Joint Photographic Experts Group — the group responsible for its creation. JPEG files are fairly small in size because they are compressed. JPEG compression is variable. You can choose to use minimal compression to very extreme compression. JPEG compression is considered a **lossy** compression scheme. When minimal compression is applied, JPEG quality remains high. However, the more a JPEG image is compressed, the more information is lost and the more image quality degrades. That is what is meant by lossy. Highly compressed JPEG files contain less information and don't look as good as minimally compressed or uncompressed files. These graphics are appropriate for web pages, because their smaller size allows them to load faster. However, graphics that are acceptable on websites often look unacceptable when they are printed. And once information has been thrown out, it can't be reclaimed.

At a minimal compression level, JPEG graphics can look quite good. But, even minimally compressed JPEGs can occasionally exhibit compression artifacts such as wavy edges in areas of photographs. This is another reason why RAW files are a better digital camera option.

In order to maximize the quality of your graphics output, never edit JPEG files. Instead, first make a copy of the JPEG file obtained from your digital camera and save it as a TIFF or PSD. By beginning your editing process with a copy, you prevent the possibility of making inadvertent permanent changes to your original file. A pristine original will be available in case you ever need to access it. Because JPEGs are a lossy format, if you resize or crop your image, the compression will be recalculated. Rather than subject your image to repeated recompressions, save it in a non-destructive file format.

Two commonly used file formats are PSD and TIFF. The first is an acronym for Photoshop Document. The second is an acronym for Tagged Image File Format. Both are good loss-less alternatives to the JPEG format. Save your JPEG original as a PSD, prior to editing if you use Photoshop or Photoshop Elements. This format works well with a range of Adobe products.

Most raster graphics programs can open TIFF formatted files. Some software programs offer the option to optimize TIFF files for either PC or Macintosh formats.

Another format, **EPS** for **Encapsulated PostScript**, should be mentioned. Conversion to EPS is sometimes required prior to submitting a graphic for commercial printing. However, conversion to **PDF**, or **Portable Document File**, with Adobe Acrobat, has largely replaced the need for EPS conversion.

Two additional paint formats are commonly used in web graphics. These are PNG and GIF. Portable Network Graphics (PNG) files, have become popular due to their small size. Unlike JPEGs, however, they are not a lossy format. They work fine for finished output, but TIFF and PSD are more useful for image editing.

Originally introduced by CompuServe, GIF files were small enough for displaying fast-loading online graphics. Additionally, they can be saved as simple animations. Their drawback, however, is that they are only capable of displaying 256 colors, which makes them useful for simple images but not for photographs.

Sizing up graphics

Film has its limitations. As a negative is enlarged, the grain begins to show, and any imperfections become more apparent. The only way to ensure great looking enlargements is to take photographs with large format cameras that use larger sheets of film (4" x 5," for example).

The same concept holds true when the photographic process captures images digitally rather than on film. Here the problem is caused by pixels rather than film grain.

As you enlarge a digital image, your photo editing software has to supply pixels that weren't originally present. It does this by sampling the surrounding pixels and taking an educated guess at what's needed. Generally photo editing software does a good job of re-sampling — as long as you don't try to over-enlarge an image. Just how much is too much, can only be answered subjectively. My personal answer is that Photoshop can double the size of an image with a resolution of 300 **pixels per inch** (**ppi**), but that's the enlargement limit unless you use a specialized enlargement program.

Image size reduction is less destructive than size enlargement, but some image degradation can still occur. Use Photoshop's **Bicubic Smoother** setting to enlarge an image and its **Bicubic Sharper** setting to reduce an image.

When working with images, always consider how they will be used. Inkjet printers can typically give good results with image resolutions of as low as 200 ppi, but higher resolutions should be used when sending an image to a LaserJet printer or to a commercial printing company. A resolution of 300 ppi is considered optimal for commercial printing. As a best practice, I always work at 300 ppi or somewhat higher.

Sizing for screen and web pages

Most computer monitors display images at either 72 ppi (McIntosh) or 96 ppi (Windows). When preparing images for screen or web presentation, either of these settings are appropriate, although 72 ppi is the most common.

Microsoft Word 2007 offers several picture compression options depending on whether a document is in the legacy DOC or newer DOCX format.

The options for DOCX documents are:
220 ppi for print
150 ppi for screen or projection
96 ppi for email

In my view, 220 ppi is too low a resolution for commercial printing; 150 ppi is unnecessarily large for screen viewing; 96 ppi is too small for acceptable output if an email is to be printed.

Typically, HTML code specifies image size. For example, "WIDTH=216 HEIGHT=432" indicates that a screen displaying 72 pixels per inch will size the image to 3" wide by 6" long. This is important to remember when using web applications such as Facebook and Blogger to display images. If your image is smaller than the specified size, it may be stretched to fit, giving a choppy, **pixilated** appearance. If it is larger than the size specified, it will be shrunk to fit the allowed space. It takes longer to download a large image and, of course, the internet is all about speed. Supplying a large image when a smaller one will do increases the time your viewer is forced to wait for your page to load. Impatient viewers will click away from slow loading pages, so don't slow your load times with unnecessarily large graphics.

Fortunately, it's easy to determine what size an image occupies on a web page. Performing a right mouse click on an image and selecting Properties, in either Firefox or Internet Explorer, opens an information box which displays an image's dimensions and other properties.

If you must work in a small space, use images that are simple — that emphasize what is important, without overburdening the viewer with obscure details. Use cropping to focus on the part that makes your point — lose the extraneous parts.

People often assume that high resolution images are not necessary since their graphics are only displayed on the web. However, occasions can arise when the same images are also needed for printed materials. Those who fail to anticipate the need for high resolution versions of images can cause themselves unnecessary difficulties. Always begin with the highest resolution images available. Downsize copies for the web, but never downsize your original images. You can always subtract pixels, but you can never fully regain information once it has been discarded.

Photo editing

Not surprisingly, the first rule of editing is to copy your original and save it with a new name. For example, if your original is named, *waterfoul-origin.tif*, name your copy something like *waterfoul-edit1.tif*. As you edit, you may find that you like a version but are not sure it's going to be your final version. Again, the solution is to make copies. You can save a version of *waterfoul-edit1.tif*, as *waterfoul-edit2.tif*. You'll now have two versions of your edited file and your original file.

Of course, you won't want to make a new copy of your image every time you make minor changes, and you won't have to. Most photo editing applications provide a means of correcting mistakes. In Photoshop, the **History Palette** helps you to undo previous operations. For example, the **Healing Brush Tool** is useful for removing scratches from old photos, but it sometimes creates undesirable results. As you use the Healing Brush, review your work frequently. Use the History Palette, to delete your errors as if they'd never occurred.

The **Layers Palette** is a similarly useful tool. Layers can be created both as empty workspaces and as copies of the base, or current layer's, image. When you create a new image, you can choose to give it either a white, colored, or transparent background. However, when you open an unedited photo, the first, or background, layer will be opaque. If you use the **Eraser Tool** on this layer, an opaque white will remain. However, if you copy the **background layer** and use the Eraser Tool, the erased area will be transparent.

There are two good reasons to always work on a copy of the background layer: 1) when you edit a copied layer, the original layer is preserved in case you ever need to refer to the unedited image, 2) since the background of your copied layer is transparent, it becomes easier to select and reposition portions of the image. There are

Figure 21. Image prior to knocking out the background

Figure 22. A knock out created from the previous image

other advantages to being able to preserve a foreground image on a transparent background —often called a **knock out** (**figures 21., 22.**). These include the ability to emphasize an object by eliminating a cluttered background, the ability to place images in montage, and the ability to use multiple copies of an image in a composition. Keep this in mind the next time you browse a magazine and you may be surprised at how often you see knock outs used in advertisements and illustrations.

The film industry has long used a technique known as blue screen, or green screen, compositing. The colored screen against which the actors are filmed is later replaced with a different background in this commonly used technique for generating special effects. The same idea can be applied when photographing products or models, in order to add a background later, or remove the background entirely. Any background color that contrasts with your subject can be easily removed in programs like Photoshop.

You can knock out areas directly on layers or by using **masks**. There are several ways to mask out areas in Photoshop. Create masks with the brush tool, or one of three lasso tools and two wand tools. Knock outs can have hard or feathered edges. I use hard edges when I need to preserve a completely transparent background. Feathered edges work well for blending selections into opaque backgrounds. Although it is possible to color correct portions of an image with masks, it is not always advisable. In some cases, after a masked area is corrected, the remainder of the image takes on a false appearance. In such cases, it's better to strive for a pleasing overall appearance instead. Sometimes however, it makes sense to mask out highlight and shadow areas in order to enhance details.

Some users adjust images in the **Levels dialog** by setting black to eight instead of zero, and white to 247 instead of 256. This preserves details in the shadow and highlight regions. On many occasions, I've improved photos by selecting a black point in a known deep shadow area in the **Curves dialog**.

Planning your project and getting it press ready

"Begin with the end in mind," writes Stephen R. Covey. Although his words summarize a broader principal, to me they describe how to implement a graphics project. Let's suppose you report to a superior who asks you to produce a star-shaped brochure. Keeping the end in mind, you approach your preferred printer for a quote. When you ask the customer service representative why his quote seems so steep, he explains that your project uses a lot of paper because of its unusual shape. It also involves more trimming than is typical. He additionally mentions that if you want envelops for your brochure, they will need to be specially fabricated by an outside vendor. "Okay," you ask, "how much will it be if the design is somewhat more conventional?"

Quotes in hand you return to your superior and ask, "How much were you planning to spend on this project?" When he tells you, you show him the quotes for the exotic and conventional brochures. Disappointed because he can't have a star-shaped brochure, but relieved that the brochure won't cost a fortune, your superior selects the more conventional brochure design.

So far you haven't even begun to design the brochure. However, you've determined the project's parameters and by doing so prevented a great deal of wasted time and expense. Granted star-shaped brochures are a little unusual, but even conventional printing looks better if you can anticipate and prevent common problems.

Let's assume that you got your brochure printed and your next project is an eight page catalog. Once again you approach your favorite printer. When you ask how many paper sheets he plans to use per catalog, he replies that he intends to use only one. Then he explains that he plans to print four pages on each side of a 17½" x 22½" sheet which he'll cut and trim into a catalog.

In most cases, the best place to spread an image across two pages is by placing the image on the two pages that occupy the publication's center. This location varies depending on how many pages are in the document. Let's suppose that you are designing an eight page catalog and want to spread an image across two of its pages. You ask your printer, "Can I put a picture across pages two and three?" He shows you a **folding dummy** and you decide to put the image across pages four and five instead (**Figure 23.**). Why?

The folding dummy shows that pages two and three are printed on the same side of the paper, so variations in ink coverage aren't a problem. However, when the paper is cut, pages two and three will be on separate sheets. If there is a slight variation in sheet size, or minor misalignment of the catalog's folded pages, then the printing won't look its best. However, by putting the picture on pages four and five, both potential problems are avoided.

The sheet size your printer will use can vary depending on both your document's size and on your printer's press size. Depending on whether your printing is done in North America or elsewhere, common paper sizes can vary as well. In North America the 8½" x 11" letter is the most common page size. Elsewhere in the world the 8¼" x 11¾" A4 page size is the most common.

Paper is supplied in sheets that are multiples of common page sizes. In North America common sheets include:
8½" x 11" letter – one page per side
11" x 17" – two pages per side
12" x 18" – two pages per side. Typically used by digital printers
17½" x 22½" – four pages per side
23" x 35" – six pages per side

Looking again at the folding dummy, a question arises. Since the pages are not printed in the same order and orientation in which they are read, does that mean you should design your document to look like the folding dummy? The answer is no. Design your document so that it's in reading order. Set the page size in your desktop publishing software to the same size as the trimmed pages will be after printing and finishing. There's a reason why I said *trimmed* pages rather than simply pages. Several of the paper sheet sizes listed above are larger than the multiples of their trimmed page sizes. One of the reasons for this is to allow an edge to be gripped while printing. Another reason is to allow room for bleeds.

Flip through any color magazine and there will be pages having pictures that are printed to the edge of the page. Despite appearances, the ink doesn't stop when it reaches the paper's edge — it goes slightly beyond the edge. The designer positions the picture slightly beyond (perhaps ⅛" beyond) where the paper will be trimmed. This area is called the **bleed**. Because ink needs to be absorbed into paper and can't simply stop at the paper's edge, bleeds are placed in areas that will be trimmed from the finished page.

Generally your desktop publishing software should have its page size set to the size your page will be after trimming. If you plan to use bleeds, you should also adjust your settings for those. Illustrator, however, does not offer a bleed option. Graphics are trimmed at the edge of the Illustrator artboard. One solution to this problem is to set the artboard dimensions to include a bleed area and place your illustrator file within an inDesign document. If your publishing software doesn't accept Illustrator files, export your file as Encapsulated Postscript or output it as an Acrobat PDF (preferable when possible). Avoid exporting as Windows Metafiles (WMF) or Enhanced Metafiles (EMF) since these do not print well.

Imposition

When a commercial printer prepares a document for printing, he arranges each page so that it will be properly positioned on the printed sheet. This arrangement process is called **imposition**. At one time performed by skilled film strippers, imposition is now typically

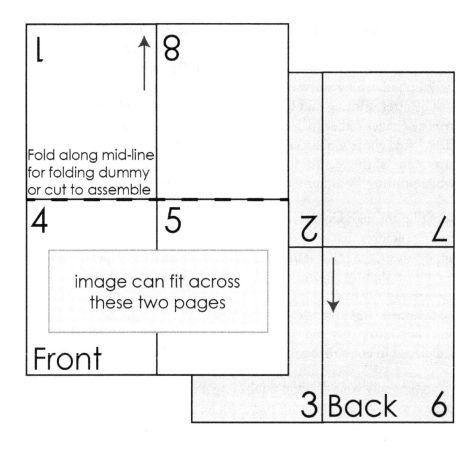

Figure 23. Page imposition for an eight page document printed on a large sheet. After printing, document is trimmed, cut, folded and assembled.

performed with Acrobat plug-in software. Despite improved technology, mistakes and miscommunications can still occur. That's why you should supply your printer with a hand assembled dummy of your document, and he should supply you with a proof before the job is printed.

Although imposition generally doesn't concern a SOHO graphics creator, there may be a few times when a little knowledge can help.

Suppose your organization doesn't need many business cards, or simply wants to test out a design before going to the expense of printing cards in bulk. In such cases it makes sense to print them yourself on perforated business card stock available from office supply stores. This card stock is often supplied with design templates for use with popular software. However, if you attempt to print artwork with a bleed on such stock, you're likely to encounter problems if your bleed area overlaps part of your printed area.

One solution is to impose your design so that the bleed areas touch across the perforation in the center of the page (**Figure 24.**). First align the business cards on the right hand side of the page. Once they are aligned, select the cards as a group and copy them. After pasting the copied cards, rotate the group 180° and butt the group against the card group on the right side of the page.

Along with perforated business card stock, tri-panel brochure stock is also available in office supply stores. Note the placement of the folds so that you can lay out your artwork accordingly. If you plan to create a tri-panel brochure and have it commercially printed, be sure to ask where the stock will be scored for folding. Different printers may have different bleed and scoring requirements, so don't just assume — ask your printer. He may tell you to mark the inside page of your tri-fold brochure so that the panels break at 22 ½ picas and at 44 ½ picas(**Figure 25.**). This means that the panels dividing the 11 inch dimension (66 picas) of your brochure will have a 22 ½ pica panel on the left which will fold over the 22 pica center panel. The smaller 21 ½ pica right panel will tuck under the left panel. If you designed your tri-fold brochure with equally sized panels, it would never fold flat. But since you placed your panel folds properly, the panels will nest inside each other and your brochure will fold flat.

Trapping

Like page imposition, **trapping** is another process that you should be aware of but may never have to deal with. Before the advent of computer graphics, trapping was a tedious task performed by skilled professionals. Today trapping is performed by pre-press technicians who use software to perform a once manual task. Being aware of graphic situations which may require trapping can help you save unnecessary pre-press costs and avoid undesired appearances in your printed output.

In conventional printing, problems sometimes occur when different colored objects touch. If the objects are not precisely aligned (misregistered), there can be unattractive gaps between them. A number of factors can cause misalignment, including press tolerances and conditions, as well as variances in paper quality, moisture, pressure, and temperature. When paper runs multiple times through high speed presses, proper trapping can minimize the effects of material and equipment variations. However, if you print with an inkjet or color laser printer, paper only passes through the printer once, so trapping is not an issue.

In a typical trap, the lighter color extends somewhat into the area occupied by the darker color. During printing, the darker color prints over the lighter, preventing gaps between the colors. Another technique is to leave intentional white space between colors, thus eliminating the need to create a trap.

When color separations are produced using PostScript, the background color will contain a knockout in the area where the overlapping color will fit. If no traps are used, and misregistration occurs during printing, an unprinted gap, called a flash, may be present between the two colors.

There are two types of traps: **chokes** and **spreads** (**Figure 26.**). When the background is darker, the lighter foreground color should overlap the background slightly. This is called a spread. When the foreground color is darker, the background color should overlap the foreground slightly. This is called a choke.

When both the foreground and background colors share the same ink, no trapping is needed. For example, if the foreground color is green and the background color is yellow, then no trap is required because both green and yellow share the same ink — yellow.

In the past, designers frequently performed the tedious chore of trapping. Thanks to digital pre-press processes, tasks like paste up and trapping have largely been eliminated. Graphics projects are frequently prepared for printing plate creation or digital printing with **raster image processors (RIPs).** These create high-resolution images from PDFs, EPS files and other graphics files. In most cases, trapping is done within RIPs, but there may be special cases requiring more hands on trapping. Some of the older RIPs do not handle transparencies well, so it's wise to ask your printer's representative if your project requires any special pre-press work.

Some graphics software offers trapping capabilities, while it is limited or non-existent in other software. Microsoft Publisher, for example, does not perform trapping unless you choose to print color separations. The trapping model Publisher uses depends on whether you are using spot or process colors. Publisher offers the capability for setting trapping thresholds in its automatic trapping dialog.

It's wise to ask your printer's representative what formats he can accept. Some printers may request that you submit your project as an inDesign file, but most will ask for a PDF. If you own Acrobat, always ask your printer which PDF format and settings he prefers.

Graphics Essentials for Small Offices

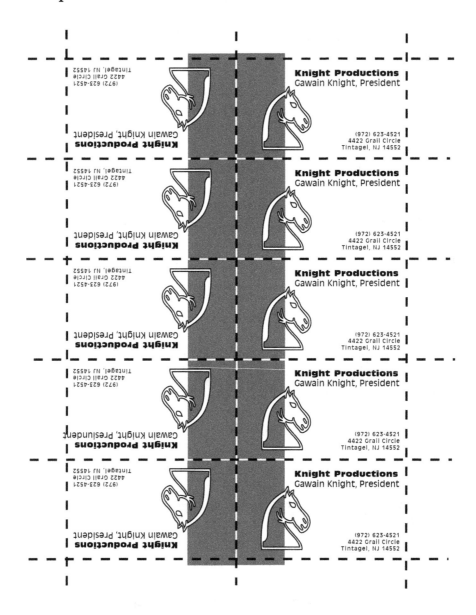

Figure 24. Imposition of business cards with left side bleed

72

Typically he'll request that you save your file as PDF/X-1a. Be sure to specify the correct bleed settings in Acrobat Distiller.

If you embed your fonts in your PDF, you needn't worry that your printer doesn't have the correct fonts. Sometimes, however, different fonts can share the same name. In rare instances, RIPs can misinterpret a font name and substitute an incorrect font. If you subset fonts when embedding fonts, Acrobat creates unique font names, preventing inadvertent substitutions. However, if you submit several PDFs, there's a possibility that when your printer combines these files, font errors will occur. Your printer can advise you on the files he can accept. Just the same, request a proof prior to printing.

Digital versus conventional printing

If there's a "take away" in the last section, it's that conventional printing requires a fair amount of pre-press planning and preparation. Digital printing avoids, or minimizes, much of the pre-press work. If you have your own digital printing equipment, you'll see results immediately instead of when a conventional printer returns a proof. Because you control every step of your workflow, errors can be quickly corrected and won't incur new charges. One downside is that you are limited to a narrow range of page sizes unless you invest in high end equipment. Such an investment is not a viable option for many SOHO organizations. Another downside is that digital printing does not offer the savings for large printing runs which are possible with conventional printing.

If, however, your printing needs are minimal, then digital printing can be a viable alternative to conventional printing. For example, if you wanted to print 25 copies of a commemorative booklet, the cost would be prohibitive with conventional printing. However, the costs would be within reason if you use a **Print on Demand** (also called **Publish on Demand**, or **POD**) company like Lulu.com or Createspace.com.

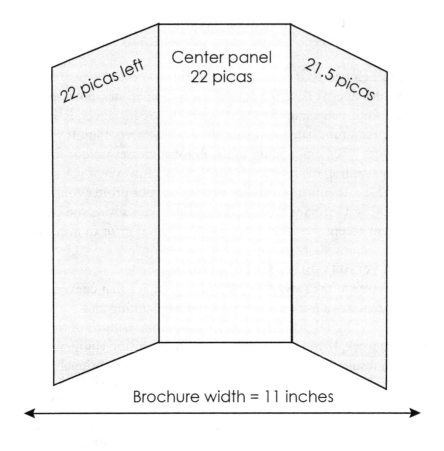

Figure 25. Panel measurements and folds for a three panel brochure

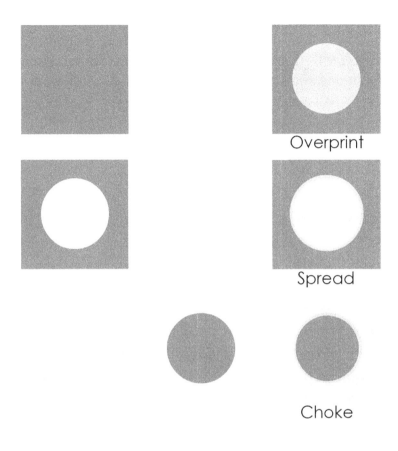

Figure 26. Overprinting versus trapping with spreads and chokes

Graphics Essentials for Small Offices

Another drawback to conventional printing is the requirement to use a CMYK color space. Most SOHO printing equipment readily accepts RGB input, as do many POD printing companies. Although a wide variety of products and sizes are available through POD printers, many finishing options such as spot varnishes or foil embossing, are not. Although companies like Lulu.com can't offer die cutting or custom sizing, they do offer a strong range of binding options.

Glossary

Alignment/text alignment The relationship of text to a page's margins, or its midline, is referred to as alignment. There are four basic alignments: **left**, **right**, **centered** and **justified**. Text that is aligned against the left margin is also referred to as **flush left**, or **ragged right**. **Flush right**, or **ragged left**, are the terms used to describe text aligned to the right margin. Centered text is aligned so that each half of the text falls equally to the right and left of the page's midline. Justified text occupies the entire line width from the left margin to the right margin. Typically the spacing between words is adjusted to achieve justified text.

anti-aliasing A process that minimizes the jagged appearance of diagonal, or curved, lines within bitmapped images. The color, or colors, composing edges within images are blended with their adjacent colors, thus creating an illusion of smooth lines.

ascender On lower case letters, such as b, d, k and h, the portion which stands above the main body of the letter is called the ascender. The ascender on a t is typically not as tall as the ascenders on other letters.

background layer When an image containing a single layer is loaded in Photoshop and similar programs, this layer can be considered the background layer. Prior to modifying an image, it's a good practice to make one (or more) duplicates of the background layer. By modifying only duplicates of the background layer, the original image information is preserved in case it is required for future reference.

Bicubic Sharper The setting Photoshop recommends be used when reducing the size of an image.

Graphics Essentials for Small Offices

Bicubic Smoother The setting Photoshop recommends be used when increasing the size of an image.

bilateral symmetry As used in design, is a process of arranging textual or graphic elements against the center of the page so that each half of an object spatially mirrors its other half. In the anatomy of animals, bilateral symmetry occurs frequently, as in eyes, hands, or kidneys placed in mirror positions to one another as measured from a midline. The appeal of bilateral symmetry may derive from its frequent appearance in nature.

bitmap/bitmap graphics (paint graphics, raster graphics) Bitmap graphics, composed of dots, or **pixels**, provide the best means of capturing continuous images such as photographs. Unlike **vector**, or **draw** graphics, their quality tends to degrade with resizing.

bleed A small printed area on a paper sheet which extends beyond the dimensions of the page after trimming. The bleed prevents a poor looking page edge by allowing printing to extend slightly past the page's edge.

cap height Refers to the height of a capital letter in a particular font. In most cases, the cap height is not as tall as the ascenders of the font's lower case letters.

CMYK An abbreviation for the four colors: cyan, magenta, yellow and black. These are the four ink colors most commonly used in full-color **offset printing**. These are also called **process colors**.

cold type (phototype) Refers to type produced through an optical process, i.e. phototypeset. Typesetting is now a digital, rather than photographic process.

color space A term used to describe an available range of colors. A computer monitor uses an **RGB** color space while color offset printing uses the **CMYK** color space. Typically digital images are converted from RGB to CMYK before being sent for **offset**

printing. Those colors which fall outside of an available color range are considered out of **gamut**. There are several photo correction tools available to compensate for out of gamut colors.

corporate identity manual Describes how an organization presents itself graphically. The manual may contain examples of acceptable logo variations and colors, examples of letterheads, envelopes and business cards, as well as the fonts and font colors that are authorized for use.

curves dialog Identical to the Photoshop levels dialog except in the manner in which information is presented.

crystallographic symmetry This type of symmetry is created through the use of repeating patterns of graphic objects. The objects may touch or be separated by white space. In either case they will be evenly distributed throughout the graphic workspace. Crystallographic symmetry is often used in the design of gift-wrap and wallpaper.

descender On lower case letters, such as g, p and q, the part which descends below the baseline of the letter is called the descender.

digital printing The direct printing of a digital image. Unlike traditional printing, in which an image is first transferred to a printing plate, or similar intermediate device, digital printing typically uses a computer, or computer based device such as a FIERY server, to output an image directly to an inkjet or LaserJet printer. Digital printing is economical when either quick results or small printing runs are needed. However, traditional printing is cheaper when a print run is large.

DPI (dots per inch) A measurement commonly used when discussing inkjet or LaserJet output, but sometimes used synonymously, if inaccurately, to mean pixels per inch (PPI). For example, scanner software may measure image capture settings in

DPI, however the captured image will be displayed in pixels. A dot of ink can only be one color, however a pixel typically displays a combination of one of 256 possible levels of red, blue or green. Therefore, it takes far fewer pixels than ink dots to display a visually pleasing image.

Draw/draw graphics (vector graphics) Computer programs can describe graphics in two ways — either as geometrical objects such as lines, angles and points, or as dots exactly positioned on the workspace. When graphics are described geometrically, they are draw or vector graphics. Draw graphics can be resized without suffering degradation since they consist of geometrical descriptions rather than fixed locations. However, **paint graphics** are more useful for capturing continuous images such as photographs.

driver A driver is a software program that interprets computer output for external devices. A display driver tells your computer's graphics card how to output video to its monitor. A print driver sends printing instructions to your printer.

embed One of two actions that can be performed with **OLE (Object Linking and Embedding)**. When an object, such as a drawing, is **embedded** in a document, it becomes a part of the document. Unlike an **embedded** object, a **linked** object can be further edited using the program in which it was created.

Encapsulated PostScript (EPS) This file format is used to translate a finished graphic into a PostScript file so that it may be displayed in non-compatible software or sent to graphics output devices such as laser printers for digital printing, imagesetters for film output, or platesetters for offset printing.

file extension The characters that follow the main portion of a file name. These characters are used to describe the file's purpose. Many file extensions are in use. Here are three examples: the extension "rtf" describes a file as "rich text format," a format recognizable by word processors. Adobe Illustrator files are designated by an "ai" extension. "Hypertext Markup Language," a format used to author web pages, can use either of two extensions: "htm" or "html."

folding dummy A folded press sheet used to indicate how a printing job will look after printing and prior to cutting and assembly. Miniature folding dummies are used to mock-up magazines and other publications.

gamut Refers to a range of colors, while **out of gamut** refers to those colors which are outside that range. In general usage, gamut refers to the colors that fall within the capability of **CMYK** inks. Since the **RGB color space** is larger than the **CMYK color space**, RGB images often contain colors that can't be accurately printed. Both Photoshop and Corel Photo-Paint provide a means of previewing the colors which will be out of gamut when printed. Additionally, Photoshop provides four methods of replacing out of gamut colors with printable ones.

graphics Can refer to anything represented visually, such as a drawing, painting or photograph. It can also be used to refer to the visual component of printed, or otherwise displayed, communication. For example a particular communication can have both a textual component and a graphic component — which in some cases may consist only in how the text is displayed, while in other cases it may involve textual attributes, illustrations and flourishes.

halftone Refers to a method of printing a continuous tone image, and to the finished output of that method. Halftones are created by reimaging a continuous tone image, i.e. photograph, through a screen of vertical and horizontal lines. The resulting image consists of dots which vary in size depending on the tone densities of the original image. In the printed image, darker or more saturated areas will have larger dots than will lighter or less saturated areas.

Graphics Essentials for Small Offices

Healing Brush Tool This is one of several image correction tools offered in Photoshop. The tool samples pixels adjacent to those which require healing and replaces them with pixels matching the area surrounding the area to be healed. It is a robust, though not perfect, image correction tool.

History Palette Although most programs provide several levels of **Undo** using the key combination **Ctrl-Z** to quickly erase mistakes, the Photoshop History Palette is unique in that it describes a series of previous states and allows the user to select among them. Use the Performance section of the Preferences settings to set the maximum number of states which the History Palette can store.

hot type Refers to type created by pouring molten metal into molds. Hot type was replaced by an optical process, known as **cold type**. Cold type was in turn replaced by a digital process thanks to computer technology.

hue Any color at its purest or most saturated level.

Imposition Commercial printers typically print on large paper sheets. After printing, these sheets are cut, trimmed, folded, and assembled into a finished document. The process of arranging pages on large sheets is called imposition — and it assures that the fronts and backs of pages will be in the correct order for assembly after printing. Imposition is a job best left to your printer. Ask your printer about the PDF settings you should use. It is also helpful to provide your printer with a hand assembled proof copy (or **folding dummy**) of your desired finished booklet, brochure, or other document.

jaggies Are the jagged diagonal lines that are visible when a bitmapped image is displayed on a monitor lacking sufficient resolution. They also occur when images are enlarged to an inappropriate degree. Apparent jaggedness can be reduced by a process known as **anti-aliasing** that blends edge colors with adjacent colors.

kern, kerning The process of manually removing or adding space between characters to improve visual appeal. This is usually performed on headlines where appearance is more crucial than in body text. It was derived from the practice of making metal type fit more closely by notching corners on certain characters. This allowed portions of the type to fit more closely with other characters having corresponding notches.

Later when type was set photographically, kerning was performed by cutting characters from the photographic paper on which type was set and repositioning them on a **paste-up** board. Now that type is digital, most well designed fonts have kerning instructions built into frequently kerned letter pairs. Additionally, graphic and publishing software generally offers kerning options.

Knock out The process, or result of, separating the subject of an image from its background. A knocked out object can be created with either feathered or hard edges depending on whether ones intent is to blend the object into the new background, or to have it stand out against the background.

Layers Palette This Photoshop palette allows the creation of multiple image layers. These can be toggled between visible or invisible, and locked or unlocked. Using layers allows a robust and non-destructive method of modifying images or parts of images. Layers can be blended to form finished images.

layout Used as a noun, the arrangement of textual and graphics elements on a page or pages. As a verb, the act of arranging text and graphics on a page or pages.

leading Refers to the strips of lead that were formerly inserted between lines of **hot type** to increase the vertical space between lines. Today the term refers to any spacing between lines of text.

levels dialog Identical to the curves dialog except in the manner in which it presents information.

Graphics Essentials for Small Offices

ligature This word has several meanings relating to tying or binding. However, in typography it refers to glyphs or characters which combine two or more letters. Scribes used ligatures to save time while copying text. Later they were incorporated into print because typesetters saved time through their use. Examples of ligatures include: æ, ff, fl, ffi, and œ, among others.

link One of two actions that can be performed with **OLE (Object Linking and Embedding)**. When an object, such as a drawing, is **linked** to a document, it can be edited in the program that created it. An **embedded** object becomes a non-editable part of the document.

LPI Lines per inch is a measurement used for halftone screens which are used to prepare photos in many commercial printing processes. Fewer LPI is required for printing on lower quality, more absorbent paper, than for higher quality, less absorbent paper. Typically, newspaper images are printed from 85 LPI halftone screens, while high quality magazines can use up to 300 LPI screens. Although they're often used interchangeably, the terms LPI and DPI have different meanings.

lossy A term used to describe a graphics compression scheme that removes data, and therefore reduces image quality.

mask A mask can be used to reveal or hide layers or portions of layers. Once created, a mask's properties can be modified. For example, shadows can be lightened and highlights deepened through the use of masks.

megapixel A term used to describe the pixel capacity of digital cameras. A megapixel refers to an array consisting of one million pixels.

monospaced font (fixed-width font) These fonts were created for typewriters whose carriages traveled a fixed horizontal distance as each letter was typed. Because typewriters could not vary the distance between characters, every letter of a monospaced font occupied the same amount of space. Although these fonts are less elegant than variable width fonts, they are still preferred for some applications. Screenplays, for example, are generally typed in monospaced fonts.

offset printing This is a very common type of commercial press. During printing, an inked plate contacts a rubber blanket. The ink from the plate is offset onto the blanket and transferred to paper.

OLE (Object Linking and Embedding) This is Microsoft's name for its application integration technology. Applications that support OLE can be integrated with other applications through **linking** and **embedding**. When an object is linked, it retains its original character and can be edited using the program in which it was created. If a linked object is moved from its original location, the link may be lost. Some programs offer features, like InDesign's Package, to help users gather all the linked files associated with a project into one location. **Embedding** can be used to incorporate an object into a document. The embedded object will no longer be editable and the resultant size of the document will be larger than if the object had been linked.

orphan 1. A line which opens a paragraph is called an orphan when it is the last line on a page or column. 2. An orphan can also be a word, or several words, that form a short line concluding a paragraph. The excess white space appearing in an orphan line is considered unattractive by typographers.

paint/paint graphics (bitmap graphics, raster graphics)
Computer programs can describe graphics in two ways — either as geometrical objects such as lines, angles and points, or as dots exactly positioned on the workspace. Paint graphics, composed of dots, or **pixels**, provide the best means of capturing continuous images such as photographs. Unlike draw graphics, paint graphic can show degradation when reduced or enlarged in size. Overly enlarged paint graphics are often said to appear **pixellated**.

Graphics Essentials for Small Offices

paste-up The act or result of preparing photographic type and graphics into a finished form prior to printing. Typically, type and graphics were cut and glued to sturdy cardboard, such as illustration board. Although paste-up has been replaced by desktop publishing and word processing software, the terms **cut** and **paste** remain as a reminder of this more time consuming process.

PDF (Portable Document File) By providing a means of displaying and printing the output of a variety of software, the PDF file format provides a means of accessing files without having to own the software originally used to create them. Although **Acrobat** Reader is available at no cost from Adobe's website, the full version of Acrobat (or a similar application from another software publisher) is required to create PDFs. Commercial printers generally prefer to receive documents as PDF files, and often use third party Acrobat plug-ins to adapt PDFs for press output.

pixel A word derived from contracting the words "picture elements," and used to describe the smallest element of a digital image displayed on a computer monitor or captured by a scanner or digital camera. Computer monitors can be adjusted to display a range of pixel grids, such as 800 by 600, or 1024 by 768 pixels.

pixilated/pixilation Refers to the appearance of an image that has been enlarged to the point that individual pixels can be distinguished by the naked eye. Image degradation that occurs prior to noticeable pixilation can be seen as jagged diagonal lines, also called **jaggies**.

phototype (cold type) A word having several meanings but used in the current context to refer to type that has been phototypeset. Such type was optically exposed on photographic paper and chemically developed. Between the late 1960s and the end of the 1980s phototype was a popular alternative to traditional hot, or metal, type.

PPI (pixels per inch) A measurement of pixel density displayed on a computer monitor or captured by a scanner or digital camera. The term DPI is often, if imprecisely, used as a synonym for PPI.

PostScript A computer language designed to describe graphic objects so that they can be correctly output on devices such as laser printers for digital printing, imagesetters for film output, or platesetters for offset printing.

print on demand (also called **Publish on Demand, POD)** Refers to the ability to print one copy, or a low number of copies, of a publication. Prior to digital printing, very small press runs were not economical. Now there are companies that specialize in printing single, or small, quantities of books, mugs, t-shirts, etc. Although the per unit cost may be somewhat higher than the cost of printing goods in large quantities, the advantage of POD is that the buyer doesn't need to commit to large inventories of printed goods.

process color One of the four colors typically used in color printing. These colors, referred to as **CMYK** are: cyan, magenta, yellow and black. In theory, blending equal amounts of the first three colors should result in black. However, due to impurities, such a blend results in a dark brown. Therefore, black is added as the fourth ink to improve the printed representation of color.

radial/rotational symmetry Is created by grouping graphic elements around, or radiating away from, a central point.

profile Refers to the calibration of monitors, printers and scanners in order to assure predictable color output.

raster graphics (bitmap graphics, paint graphics) Computer programs can describe graphics in two ways — either as geometrical objects such as lines, angles and points, or as dots exactly positioned on the workspace. Raster graphics, composed of dots, or **pixels,** provide the best means of capturing continuous images such as photographs. Unlike draw graphics, paint graphics can show degradation when reduced or enlarged in size. Overly enlarged paint graphics are often said to appear **pixellated**.

raster image processor (RIP) 1. Software which converts **PostScript, PDF**, and other graphics file formats to high resolution data usable by an output device to create printing plates, digital printing, or similar output. 2. The term RIP can also refer to the dedicated computer, typically a server, on which the image processing software RIP resides.

registration/register In traditional multicolor printing each color must be printed separately. When the colors are properly aligned, the printed output is in register. When printing is out of register, its appearance may lack sharpness and detail, and colors may overlap one another in an unattractive manner. In cases where tight registration is difficult to achieve, such as on packaging, a technique called **trapping** is used to anticipate and compensate for registration errors.

RGB An abbreviation for the three colors: red, green and blue. Computer monitors display a combination of these three colors. Since the RGB color space displays a greater range of colors than the CMYK color space, it is generally used when a maximum color range is desired. Several variations of the RGB color range are available as color profiles, including sRGB and Adobe RGB (1998).

river Is a visual illusion of a line of white space running vertically down a paragraph. Rivers are due to poor word spacing and can be visually distracting. Rivers can occur in any text, but are most likely to occur when text is fully justified or uses monospaced fonts. Quality software is less likely to produce rivers than was traditional typesetting equipment. However, contemporary software users are less likely to check for rivers then were professional typesetters.

serif type & sans-serif type Serif fonts are distinguished by the small flourishes, or notches, that appear at the ends of their letter strokes. Those fonts which lack serifs are designated by the French word "sans" for "without."

saturation A saturated color is a color at its fullest intensity. Decreasing saturation in Photoshop or similar software results in a shade of gray.

shade A color mixed with an amount of black.

signature This is a bookbinding term for a group of printed and folded sheets intended for binding. Since press sizes vary, signatures can be of 8, 16 or 32 pages. The number of signatures used may be a factor in print pricing. For this reason, it may be useful to either increase or decrease the number of pages included in a book in order to achieve a marketable ratio between book size and selling price.

spot color A spot color is any color, other than one of the four **process colors** (**CMYK**), that is applied in a single print run. Spot colors can include named or mixed colors as well as metallic and florescent colors. The application of special finishes such as varnish also requires its own print run, and can in some ways be treated like spot colors for costing purposes.

tint This word has several meanings. When printers and designers use it, they generally mean a less than fully saturated color. Examples of tints could include: 90 percent black, 60 percent magenta and 20 percent cyan. When a painter uses the word, he generally means mixing a color with an amount of white.

tracking Unlike kerning, which refers to the spacing between individual letter pairs, tracking involves adjusting the spacing between characters in a selection of text.

trap, trapping When two colors touch in traditionally printed documents, there is a possibility that they may be out of **register**. Trapping is a technique in which one color is overlapped by another. The two types of traps are called **chokes** and **spreads**. When a lighter color is printed over a darker color, it should overlap slightly. This is called a spread. When a darker color is printed over a lighter one, its overlap chokes the lighter color by printing over its borders. While graphics printed digitally won't require traps, there may be occasions when trapping may need to be performed while preparing a job for offset printing. It's best to consult your printer during the design phase. He can advise you regarding trapping techniques or the cost of having his staff perform trapping prior to printing.

typography Pertains to the appearance of type including the spatial and stylistic relationships between individual letters, and their appearance in headlines, lines and paragraphs of type.

variable-width font (proportional font) Letters in variable-width fonts differ in the amount of horizontal space they occupy. Although more eye-pleasing than **monospaced fonts**, they are less useful in instances where vertical alignment of letters is desired.

variable data printing (VDP) Thanks to digital printing technology, VDP allows printing to be individually customized to include such personal data as the recipient's name. Although high volume VDP is more expensive than printing the same volume of identical items, it is highly effective when used for direct mail marketing.

vector graphics (draw graphics) Computer programs can describe graphics in two ways — either as geometrical objects such as lines, angles and points, or as dots exactly positioned on the workspace. Draw, or vector, graphics are described geometrically. These graphics can be resized without suffering degradation since they consist of geometrical descriptions rather than of dots occupying fixed locations. **Paint graphics**, composed of dots, are more useful for capturing continuous images such as photographs, while vector graphics are useful for designing with shapes such as lines, rectangles and ovals.

widow When a new column or page begins with the line that concludes a paragraph, that line is considered to be widow. Typographers consider widow lines unattractive due to their having an excess of white space filling out the text line.

x-height The body size of lower case letters is often referred to as their x-height. This is the height from the baseline to the top of a lower case x.

References and Recommendations

Adobe Corporation. A glossary of typographic terms. http://www.adobe.com/type/topics/glossary.html

Beadsworth, John. *Digital black and white photography: A step-by-step guide to creating perfect photos.* Boston: Course PTR, 2004.

Cohen, Sandee and Williams, Robin. *The Non-Designer's Scan and Print Book.* Berkeley: Peachpit Press, 1999.

Evans, Poppy and Sherin, Aaris. *Forms, Folds and Sizes: all the details graphic designers need to know but can never find.* Beverly, Massachusetts: Rockport Publishers, Inc., 2008.

Goldstein, Norm (Editor). *The Associated Press Stylebook and Briefing on Media Law.* Cambridge, Massachusetts: Perseus Publishing, 2002.

Kent, Lynette. *Photoshop CS5 Top 100 Simplified Tips and Tricks.* Indianapolis, Indiana: Wilely Publishing, Inc., 2010.

McCue, Claudia. *Real World Print Production with Adobe Creative Suite Applications.* Berkeley: Peachpit Press, 2009.

Peterson, Bryan L. *Design Basics for Creative Results.* Cincinnati: HOW Design Books, 2003.

Phinney, Thomas W. A Brief History of Type. http://nwalsh.com/comp.fonts/FAQ/cf_28.htm

Sheppard, Rob. *New Epson guide to digital printing.* New York: Lark Books, 2008.

Thomas, Gregory. *How to Design Logos, Symbols and Icons.* Cincinnati: North Light Books, 2000.

Graphics Essentials for Small Offices

Walker, Michael and Barstow, Neil. *The Complete Guide to Digital Color Correction.* New York: Lark Books, 2004.

Wheildon, Colin. *Type & Layout: how typography and design can get your message across, or get in the way.* Berkeley: Strathmoor Press, Inc., 1995.

White, Alexander W. *The elements of graphic design: space, unity, page architecture, and type.* New York: Alworth Press, 2002.